DEEP NATURE OBSERVATION

Arboreal Press
Hummelstown, PA 17036

ISBN-13: 979-8-9991586-9-7

First Edition: 2026
10 9 8 7 6 5 4 3 2 1

DEEP NATURE OBSERVATION

A MORE-THAN-FIVE SENSES GUIDE TO CONNECTING WITH THE OUTDOORS

Josh VanBrakle

Arboreal Press

AUTHOR'S NOTE

This book almost didn't exist.

I started work on this book in 2018. It feels like another life. Global pandemics were still the stuff of science fiction.

I got pretty far with it, too. Did tons of research. Wrote a draft. Went through several revisions.

Then 2020.

I changed jobs in January of that fateful year. I set this book down so I could focus on my new work responsibilities. Just for a couple months, I told myself. I wanted to make sure I could still balance writing with having a day job and a family.

March 2020 hit. COVID pandemic, lockdowns...you've heard that story before.

In the midst of all that chaos, I never reopened this book. It sat on my computer, forgotten.

But a friend of mine remembered it. You owe this book to her, not me. Because without her, this book never would have made it off my hard drive.

Fast forward five years. I'm standing in a hallway at work waiting for the elevator. A colleague of mine, Nicole Faraguna, happened to be waiting for the same elevator.

And she asked me about this book.

In a moment of complete embarrassment, I had to admit to her that I'd never finished it. That I doubted I ever would. That I hadn't so much as looked at it in five years.

"You should," she told me.

Two words. We took the elevator and parted. But those two words rang like a gong in me: you should.

So I did.

I reread old drafts. Explored new research. Updated ideas. Refined the language. Found a host of new photos.

Somewhere in there, the spark of writing, which I thought the pandemic had stolen from me, came back.

You're holding the result.

Nicole, if you're reading this, thank you. From the bottom of my heart, thank you. Not only for encouraging me to retrieve this book from the dustbin of my laptop, but for helping me rekindle a love of writing I feared I'd lost forever.

I have no idea what books come after this one. But for the first time since the pandemic, I'm excited to find out.

Let's get started.

TABLE OF CONTENTS

Chapter 1

SENSORY NUMBNESS

A person hears only what they understand.
– Johann Wolfgang von Goethe

In 1999, psychologists Christopher Chabris and Daniel Simons conducted one of the strangest human behavior experiments of all time.

They brought participants at Harvard University into a room one by one and had them sit in front of a TV. The psychologists put on a video of basketball players standing in a circle and tossing a ball back and forth. Some players had black shirts. Others had white shirts.

The participants' job was simple. Count the number of times the white shirts passed the ball.

Except here's the thing. That wasn't actually their job. Counting basketball throws had nothing at all to do with the study. In further proof that you should never believe anything a psychology researcher tells you, the basketball tossing was merely a distraction.

Partway through the video, a person in a gorilla suit walks on-screen. The gorilla walks between the basketball players, stands in the middle of the circle, beats his chest, then walks out of frame.

When the video ended, the researchers asked the participants,

"Did you notice anything odd about the video?" And an astonishing thing happened.

Half the participants replied, "No."

Let that sink in. A person in a gorilla suit walked right through the center of the video frame, and half the people watching missed it completely.

The experiment became one of the most famous in psychology. To this day, it's known as the Invisible Gorilla Experiment.

The Invisible Gorilla has no subliminal trickery. The gorilla is in frame for nine seconds in a video that lasts less than forty. Don't believe me? Watch the video yourself at www.theinvisiblegorilla.com.

What happened here? How could people miss something so obvious?

The problem wasn't with their eyes. It was in their minds. The answer comes down to attention.

Attention sounds like a good thing. We admonish children, "Pay attention!" when they knock something over. We value "attention to detail" in our work so we don't make careless mistakes.

Attention is a valuable trait.

Properly applied, we call it "concentration" and use it to achieve amazing things. You're using concentration right now to read these words. I used concentration to write them.

But attention can also become problematic. Our modern world has warped attention into a never-ending, laser-like focus. Ads compete to draw our eye from other ads. Everyone on social media is screaming, "Look at me! I'm so amazing!" Endless pings and notifications tell us about all the texts, posts, and likes we're missing.

In this technology-driven quest for our attention, we become overloaded. We never zoom back out and take in the bigger picture. All we do is shift from one tiny window to another.

This loss of the broader world is what the Invisible Gorilla experiment revealed. Participants focused so narrowly—on the movement of the ball—that they literally missed the gorilla right in front of them.

We do this all the time without realizing it. When you stare at your cell phone screen, the entire world disappears at the phone's edge. Your vision tunnels until your whole existence is the phone.

That's a terrifying thought. It's made all the more terrifying when you think about all the people walking and driving while staring into their phones.

Sometimes our tunnel vision isn't even to something external. We can become so obsessed with our internal, looping thoughts that we stop paying attention to the outside world completely. Did I shut the garage door this morning? What will go wrong at work today? What are

The days when we needed to spot lions in savanna grass may be over, but that doesn't mean we have to lose the keen senses we possess for taking in and enjoying the world. Photo: Mitch Mitchell on Unsplash

the kids doing after school?

We walk around in a mental fog. We dwell on the past or worry about the future while utterly missing the present.

Psychologists refer to this tunnel vision as "inattentional blindness."

The tunnel affects more than sight. As our go-go world sucks us into ever shorter attention windows, we are gradually losing all our senses. We're tossing away our abilities to see, hear, smell, feel, and taste—and with them, our deepest, truest connections to the world.

"Inattentional blindness" doesn't do service to this loss. I call it "sensory numbness."

In sensory numbness, we don't physically lose our senses. Instead, we become inured to them. We tune them out. And then, like muscles that don't get used, they atrophy.

Why does sensory numbness happen? From an evolutionary perspective, it makes no sense. A caveman wandering the savanna in a mental haze won't see that saber-tooth tiger crouching in the tall grass. Chomp. No, the caveman survives by being present in the moment, spotting and avoiding the glinting eyes in the distance.

For thousands of years, we occupied our minds with thoughts of the present. We developed keen awareness of the rhythms and movements of nature. Our survival depended on it.

These days, we don't have to worry about saber-tooth tigers. We no longer need to track and kill our food

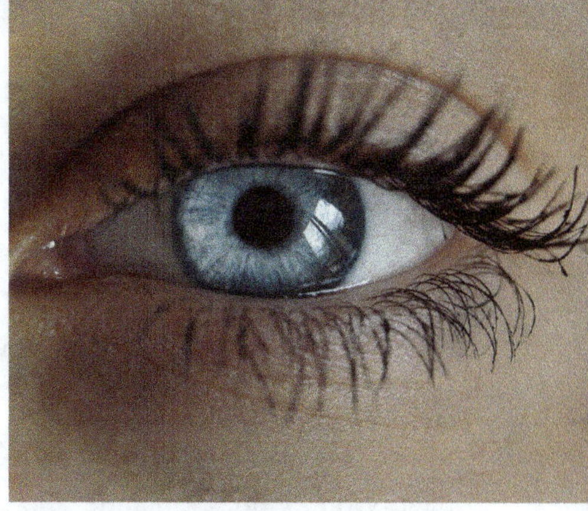

Our senses are better than we give ourselves credit for. Our color vision, for example, far exceeds that of many other mammals. Photo: Dimitar Krastev on Unsplash

or tell edible plants from poisonous ones. We don't have to determine the weather or chart direction by the movements of clouds and stars.

The result is predictable. Our senses weaken. Our world shrinks.

Where once we experienced beauty, color, music, and flavor, now we find only the same-old, same-old dullness. We believe we have "seen it all before." In the process, we miss so much of what happens right in front of us—including people in gorilla suits.

We don't have to live this way. Common wisdom says that humans have horrible senses compared to wild animals. That wisdom is wrong.

We have amazing senses. We can see more than a million shades of color. We can differentiate one trillion smells.

Sensory numbness is mental, not physical. Our physical senses are better than we give them credit for. We just don't use them. We lack observation skills and opportunities to practice them.

But you can learn these skills. That's why I wrote this book. I want to lift you out of the mental fog of your daily routine. I want to help you experience this amazing world with all your senses.

My goal in this book isn't to teach you specific natural signs, like telling direction by the North Star. Plenty of survival guides include that information. Some of those signs will inevitably come up in this book, but I view them as a side benefit.

Instead, I want to teach you broader skills that you can apply to any situation outside.

In this book you'll learn how to use wide-angle vision to process a landscape in an instant. You'll learn three-dimensional listening to pinpoint a sound's distance and direction. You'll even learn about senses beyond the five—senses that will connect you with nature in ways you never thought possible.

More than these skills, I want to teach you a mindset, a way of viewing the world that I call Deep Nature Observation. Deep Nature Observation combines all the skills in this book to defeat sensory numbness. It lets you experience the world deeply and fully, in the moment, wherever you are.

When you apply Deep Nature Observation to your time outdoors, you'll improve every moment you spend in nature, whether that moment is a walk in the park, a hike up a mountain, or a canoe journey downriver.

But why? Who needs a quaint skill like observing nature in the first place? We have online stores. We have smartphones. Perhaps we've evolved beyond the need for nature.

I don't think we have. Our survival may no longer depend on observing nature, but our health and wellness do.

Our brains despise boredom. It's the double-edged sword of having such large brains. They demand stimulation. Even if you don't need to observe the world with the detail your ancestors did, your brain still has that amazing sensory processing power. It will use it on something.

And because it no longer needs to pay attention to the external, its focus warps to the internal.

Hence, we get all those looping, worrying thoughts. The brain dwells on them, watches them like they're a lurking saber-tooth tiger.

Unlike the tiger, the brain can't "solve" those worries. It can tell the caveman to fight or flee the tiger, but it can't make you get that job, score that date, or raise the kids' grades.

Because the brain can't solve these problems, it panics. It obsesses over them, trying to solve the insolvable. That obsession leads to stress, anxiety, and depression.

Deep Nature Observation can help combat these negative thoughts. In the process, it adds a powerful tool in our health toolbox, one that can improve both our physical and mental well-being.

As we'll explore in the next chapter, a sensory-immersed experience in nature has proven health benefits for both our bodies and our minds. Multiple studies across countries and decades have shown that immersing ourselves in nature can reduce heart disease, Type II diabetes, insomnia, depression, dementia, obesity, ADHD, and even cancer. It improves memory, mood, self-esteem, creativity, teamwork, and problem solving.[1]

Best of all, these benefits are possible no matter what your experience is with the outdoors, your level of physical fitness, or how urban or rural your home is. The benefits of Deep Nature Observation are open to everyone.

Out there is not the same-old, same-old. Out there is a world of such depth, beauty, and subtlety that you could never experience it all. You could look and look and look and still find something new every day.

So however you like to enjoy nature, let this book open your eyes. And ears. And nose and mouth and hands. You have senses you didn't even know you had. Use them.

We live in a world filled with wonder. No way have we "seen it all before." Get out there and explore.
Author photo

Chapter 2

WHAT IS DEEP NATURE OBSERVATION?

I see no more than you, but I have trained myself to notice what I see.
– Sherlock Holmes

We suffer from sensory numbness. But how do we overcome it? What is Deep Nature Observation, anyway, and how do we do it?

To answer these questions, we first need to learn a little about our brains.

It turns out, we don't have just one nervous system. We have two: the "sympathetic" and the "parasympathetic."

The sympathetic nervous system has a simpler name you already know: the fight-or-flight system. It kicks in as a response to a stressful situation. From an evolutionary perspective, it prepared the body to fight for its life or run away when confronted with danger—say, that saber-tooth tiger from the last chapter.

When the sympathetic nervous system kicks in, it mobilizes you for action. Heart rate accelerates. Muscles tense. Vision tightens. Strong feelings of anger (to help you fight) and fear (to help you run) arise.

By contrast, the parasympathetic nervous system is a relaxing system. It's the system that's in control when we rest. Digestion speeds up. Heart rate and breathing slow. The senses expand to take in more. Emotionally, the parasympathetic system is responsible for feelings of love and happiness.

As I said in the last chapter, we no longer have saber-tooth tigers to worry about. But unlike our senses, which have weakened without external stimulation, our fight-or-flight system is working harder than ever. The stresses of modern life put that system into constant overdrive.

The problem with that? Our bodies aren't designed to have fight-or-flight be our normal mode. That system is meant for short bursts of activity, like self-defense.

The parasympathetic system, the relaxing system, is supposed to dominate. We need it to recover from those bursts of activity.

Because we spend so much time with the fight-or-flight system in control, we've come to think of it as normal. It's not. And this unnatural dominance of fight-or-flight explains at least some of the increased feelings of anger, fear, worry, and depression many of us feel. We never give our bodies a chance to recover, to come back to the parasympathetic system.

Deep Nature Observation offers a tool to help you do that. It gives you a break from fight-or-flight and lets the parasympathetic system drive for a while.

This approach may sound familiar if you've ever tried mindful meditation. That's on purpose. Deep Nature Observation uses some of the same concepts that meditation employs to relax and then refocus the mind.

That said, Deep Nature Observation isn't meditation per se. Instead, it's a way of reframing our outdoor experiences. It helps us focus on where we are and what we're experiencing in that moment, rather than ruminate on what we've done or worry about where we're going.

SOFT FASCINATION

That sounds great, but what does it mean, exactly? What makes Deep Nature Observation any different from a normal walk in the woods?

The difference is one of mindset. We can't truly experience nature with all our senses until we shift out of the way we interact with the world in our usual working lives.

That's harder to do than it sounds. We've become so used to our stressed out, fight-or-flight world that we've begun to think it's the only way to live.

Worse, we often scorn relaxation as "lazy" or "unproductive." That

Ironically, softening your focus outdoors is the first step to more deeply connecting with nature. Let yourself see broadly and without analysis. Ultimately, that will help you spot smaller details than you would have otherwise. Photo: Sam Di Risio on Unsplash

TRY THIS — SHINRIN YOKU

Reading through my description of Deep Nature Observation, you might be reminded of a related outdoor recreation practice: the Japanese technique of shinrin yoku, also known as "forest bathing."

Forest bathing has nothing to do with an actual bath. Rather, it's the practice of taking relaxing walks in a forest to boost your health.

Decades of research support this technique. In one project, researchers had 280 people walk both in the woods and in a city. After walking in the woods, the participants had reduced blood pressure, a slower heart rate, and lower levels of the stress hormone cortisol compared with when they walked in the city.[1]

Deep Nature Observation complements the Japanese technique of shinrin yoku, or forest bathing. Deep Nature Observation can extend your forest bathing sessions by giving your mind an activity that is both relaxing and engaging. Photo: Rebecca Clarke on Unsplash

In another pair of studies, researchers brought groups of men and women into the woods for a three-day, two-night trip. Throughout the trip, the researchers measured the level of natural killer cells in the people's bodies—an indicator of immune function. By the second day of the trip, the level of those cells had increased by more than 50 percent. More impressive, even a month later, immune function remained significantly higher than before the people spent time in the woods.[2]

So is Deep Nature Observation just another name for forest bathing? Not exactly. Both call for slowing down and letting the parasympathetic nervous system reassert itself. But as we'll see in this chapter, maintaining that mindset shift is challenging. Deep Nature Observation is deliberately designed to provide mind-filling engagement while holding the fight-or-flight system at bay.

The other key difference is location. Where shinrin yoku specifically identifies forests, you can practice Deep Nature Observation anywhere. Your backyard, a local park, even a city street are full of nature if you're willing to look closely and with an open mind.

If you already practice forest bathing, consider integrating some Deep Nature Observation into your routine. You may find that it makes it easier to maintain and even extend your forest bathing time.

Soft fascination doesn't mean you can't focus on something small. When something catches your attention, give it a close look. Don't analyze it. Just enjoy it for what it is. Then return to your broad view. Photo: Alex Gomez on Unsplash

makes the shift in mindset even harder, because we mistakenly feel like we're doing something wrong by taking a break.

Let me pause a moment to make sure I'm clear about this. You are *not* doing something wrong by slowing down. You aren't "wasting time." When you engage in Deep Nature Observation, it's impossible to waste time. Absolutely the opposite. You're learning, absorbing, and filling yourself with the world around you.

With that out of the way, the first step in switching out of fight-or-flight mode is to adjust your approach to attention.

In our daily lives, everything competes for our attention. Work, media, ads, politics…they all de-mand we focus on them.

This kind of attention is called "directed attention." Other people and messages "direct" our attention to themselves. Like the saber-tooth tiger, these outside stimuli force us to zero our focus in on them.

As a consequence, our brains never get to choose what to pay attention to. They just rush to the most immediate fire and try to put it out. Then it's off to the next issue screaming at us.

Directed attention explores one object in depth. It digs in, analyzes that object, and picks it apart.

We need to shut off that analysis during Deep Nature Observation. Instead of interpreting and judging everything that comes our way, Deep Nature Observation calls on us to accept and enjoy sensory input for what it is.

Forest bathing researcher Dr. Qing Li has described this acceptance as "soft fascination"—the simple joy that comes from appreciating the world as it is.

Ironically, then, the first step in Deep Nature Observation is to pay less attention. Instead of directing our attention to one thing in particular, we need to zoom back from our tunnel vision and take in the broader landscape.

That isn't to say you can't focus on anything. To the contrary. Suppose you hear a looping, descending song in the distance, like two musicians spiraling around each other. "That's a veery!" you exclaim, and chase after this amazing thrush.

In that moment, you're focused on that one bird. But critically, after pursuing that bird, let your attention pull back again to the landscape.

This ability to pull our attention back, rather than career from one narrow focus to another, separates soft fascination from our daily mindset. In our daily lives, our attention gets yanked in directions it doesn't want to go but feels compelled to follow. In soft fascination, we let our attention decide for itself, subconsciously, what it would like to focus on.

This back-and-forth shifting of focus is again inspired by meditation. When beginners meditate, they often think they're doing it wrong if their thoughts wander. They aren't. Experienced meditators learn to recognize wandering thoughts. Rather than feel like they've made a mistake, they simply accept their thoughts for what they are, without judgment. Then they return to the meditation.

Soft fascination works the same way. When you practice soft fascination with nature, your attention will find something it wants to watch, listen, smell, feel, or taste. Indulge that desire (within safe limits, obviously). Then return to broad observations.

ABANDON GOALS

We all have goals. Modern life—modern American life, in particular—thrives on them. We want to land that job, get that date, climb that mountain.

Goals drive us to perform, to excel, to go beyond where we are right now. Like attention and concentration, they are remarkably useful.

And also like attention and concentration, they can be remarkably self-destructive.

Goals are a product of the fight-or-flight system. They push us to focus on a narrow achievement, ignoring the world around us.

That isn't necessarily bad. After all, goals help us achieve amazing things.

When I sat down to write today, I set a goal to write 4,000 words. That

Abandoning goals doesn't mean we have to give up climbing mountains. Just remember the old saying: it's the journey, not the destination.
Photo: Alice Ruan on Unsplash

goal pushed me forward. Without goals, I would never have finished this book, or my education, or any of the other accomplishments I've had in my life.

Yet as important as goals are, it's important to realize that having them can't make us happy. And as shocking as it may be to hear, neither can achieving them.

When you're working on achieving your goal, you aren't happy. You're pushing yourself. You're using that fight-or-flight system. As we know, that system creates feelings of anger and fear. Instead of happiness, you're more likely to get frustrated at your

Approach the outdoors not with a goal but with a mindset of "I wonder what I'll discover today?" When you adopt this explorers' mind, you'll open yourself up to all kinds of experiences you never would have had otherwise. Author photo

pace of progress or become fearful that you'll never achieve what you set out to do.

What about when you achieve your goal? Shouldn't that make you happy?

Sure, for a moment. But what does society teach us? Never be satisfied. Once you've finished one goal, you want to jump on the next goal.

I wrote 4,000 words today. I have the same goal tomorrow. The happiness lasts a few minutes. Then it's back to the grind.

Just like attention, this propensity toward goals is so ingrained in our culture that it follows us into nature. We head outside hoping to climb a mountain we've never scaled before, or to add a new bird to our life list. If we don't achieve that goal, we feel disappointed.

Disappointment aside, having a goal outdoors makes Deep Nature Observation more difficult. Recall that one of the fight-or-flight system's functions is to give us tunnel vision. It deliberately blurs the background so we can focus all our attention on the saber-tooth tiger.

This tightening of our senses helps us survive against predators. But it also makes it impossible to observe the full breadth of our surroundings.

If you focus on a goal like through-hiking a trail or reaching a vista, your mind and senses will subconsciously zero in on that endpoint. In such a state, the parasympathetic nervous system can't engage and widen your field of view.

As with soft fascination, changing

The back-and-forth from soft fascination to close inspection of something interesting, like this northern slimy salamander, can fill your mind and push out frustrating ruminations. Author photo

this mindset is hard. We're so conditioned to chase goals that to abandon them feels wrong. If you aren't careful, it can even turn into a goal itself. "I will not have a goal today," you tell yourself. That's a goal!

So what do you do? Nothing.

When you step onto the trailhead, don't tell yourself anything at all. Don't say that you will see a certain number of wildflower species or hear a certain number of birds. Don't plan to take a certain trail or reach a certain destination.

Leave all your expectations back home. Let nature come to you. Let it and your subconscious mind—through soft fascination—guide your experience.

DON'T CLEAR YOUR MIND. FILL IT.

As important as soft fascination and abandoning goals are for Deep Nature Observation, they do come with the potential for a nasty side effect.

Remember, the brain abhors boredom. We often think of "relaxation" as "having nothing to do," but have you ever really had nothing to do? It isn't relaxing. It's miserable. The clock crawls. You stew. You worry.

When you slacken your attention and let go of goals, your brain will instinctively try to fill that void. And what will it fill it with? All the stresses and cares weighing you down in the first place!

This side effect trips up many people who try meditation. They think the point of meditation is to clear the mind. It isn't. Clearing the mind is only the first step. Once you clear your mind, you have to fill it.

In mindful meditation, you refill the mind with something repetitive. You may count breaths or the beads on a rosary. Maybe you say a mantra.

Even simple interactions with nature, like touching a patch of moss, can lead to profound revelations, as I discovered one evening with my daughter. Author photo

In Deep Nature Observation, we do something different. We fill our minds not with the internal, but with the external. We fill our minds with our senses.

You may be asking yourself, "But how? I don't know a lot of species. How can I notice more?"

You don't need to know a lot of species to notice more. As we'll discuss in later chapters, yes, knowing various plants and animals will help you pick them out from the background. But even if you don't know a single species name, you can still experience more than you would normally.

By abandoning goals and adopting soft fascination, you've positioned your body to experience the world with your senses in a way you never could in your daily life. You are ready to, as Sherlock Holmes put it, "notice what you see." You can use your amazing sensory processing power to become aware of nature's innumerable details that normally pass us by.

How do I know you can do this, even if you don't know any species? Because children do it every day.

I have a daughter. She teaches me more about Deep Nature Observation than any book ever could. One August evening when she was two, we were playing out on our patio. Bedtime was rapidly approaching. We were both tired. She needed a bath. All I wanted to do was get inside and start our routine.

Then she saw the moss.

We have this short brick wall at the back of our patio. Scattered moss patches grow on top of it. I ignore them, since they're small and don't seem to do any harm.

Not my daughter. This evening, she ran up to them and rubbed her hand on one. She giggled. "Soft!" she declared.

What else can I do? I felt the moss too. It reminded me of a shag carpet—dry and plush and, yes, soft.

I was in the beginning of thinking about this book that evening, and I had a revelation. How many times had I walked by that moss? Even I, someone who wanted to write a book about observing nature, hadn't seen that moss, let alone touched it.

In that moment, I realized my toddler was much more observant than I was when it comes to nature. She embodied Deep Nature Observation.

My daughter didn't judge the moss. She didn't analyze its role in the patio ecosystem. She didn't worry about where the moss came from or what would happen to it in the future. She just enjoyed it for what it was right in that moment.

For adults, such pure enjoyment is hard. We've become so jaded about the world that we forget there are simple things—like the soothing feel of moss in the palm of your hand— that we have never experienced.

I've spent this whole chapter try- ing to explain how to get to that

Kids are experts at Deep Nature Observation. Their sensory numbness hasn't kicked in yet. To forge a stronger connection with nature, embrace that childlike curiosity deep inside you. Photo: Lê Hong on Unsplash

enjoyment, but in the end, it comes down to one step. Want to observe nature more? Become a child.

That's what I'm asking you to do in this book. The mindset of Deep Nature Observation is the mind not of a naturalist, but of a child.

Like a child, it's important not to judge yourself in this observing. My daughter wasn't bothered that she didn't know what moss was. Nor was she upset that in exploring the moss, she missed the other plants growing in the garden nearby. Deep Nature Observation is taking in nature at a moment in time and accepting it for what it is without analysis or judgment.

You aren't trying to see everything. That's impossible. Actually, that's to your benefit. It means you can keep returning to the same place and always experience something new.

The point of Deep Nature Observation is simply to experience more with your senses than you would have otherwise. Did you hear a bird you would have missed if you'd been hiking at full speed? That's success. Did you see that deer hiding behind the bush, hoping its camouflage would render it invisible? That's success too!

And even if you didn't hear that bird or see that deer, did you enjoy the moment, simply feeling the breeze on your cheeks and smelling the deep aroma of the pines? That's

Deep Nature Observation.

The skills I describe in the rest of this book will help you observe more in nature. But they'll only be as useful as your ability to shed your tightly focused, goal-oriented perspective and adopt the child's view of the world.

Happiness isn't found at the top of a mountain or the end of a trail. It's found in the way the morning sun glints off an egret's white wings as it lands in a marsh. It's found in the way the first spring wildflowers push themselves up through the cold earth and turn the forest floor alive with color. It's found in the stories told around a campfire as you gaze into the endless night sky.

It's taken me more than 2,000 words in this chapter to define Deep Nature Observation. Perhaps to close, I'll let a poet do a far better job than I have using just 16:

"TO SEE A WORLD IN A GRAIN OF SAND
AND A HEAVEN IN A WILD FLOWER."

– WILLIAM BLAKE
"AUGURIES OF INNOCENCE"

That is Deep Nature Observation. The poets and toddlers are already there. The rest of this book will help you and me catch up.

I think this William Blake fellow may be onto something. Also, now I really want to go to the beach.
Photo: Frank McKenna on Unsplash

Chapter 3

PREPARING TO OBSERVE

To find new things, take the path you took yesterday.
— John Burroughs

The last chapter explored mentally how we can become more aware of our senses. Now we shift to physical matters.

Keeping that mindset of open, relaxing time in nature, the next several chapters delve into the skills that will help you exploit that mindset to get more out of your outdoor experiences. Each chapter in this section is devoted to a particular sense and lays out skills that can help you apply that sense more effectively.

Before we talk about the senses themselves, let's spend a little time on the art of observation itself. Just as there are techniques to hone your sensory skills, there are practices you can use to improve your overall nature-based experiences.

If you've spent a lot of time outdoors, some of these topics will feel like review. It's worth revisiting them, though. A conscious effort to prepare for time in nature will train your mind to separate outdoor recreation from your usual fast-paced experience. When you start packing your daypack or looking up a trail map, your mind will recognize that as the start of a routine—a relaxing routine. By the time you reach the trailhead, you'll be that much closer to freeing yourself of the fight-or-flight mindset and adopting a Deep Nature Observation one.

PLACE

Place might seem like an odd topic. After all, in earlier chapters I mentioned how Deep Nature Observation is something anyone can do no matter where you live.

To be sure, Deep Nature Observation works in any outdoor spot, whether that's a remote mountain or the vacant lot down the street. That's why I chose the John Burroughs quote to start this chapter. If you open yourself up to your senses, even the paths you've long trodden can offer new insights.

That said, some parks and forests lend themselves more readily to nature observation. First, look for places with gentle slopes. It's harder to focus on small details if you're heaving for every breath as you crawl up a mountainside.

Similarly, seek well-marked and maintained trails. Since Deep Na-

In the Catskill Mountains where my wife and I used to live, we walked the same nature trail almost weekly for seven years. In the fall before we moved, we were both startled by a mass of insects swarming on a wooden fence along the trail. The creatures were boxelder bugs—harmless herbivores that eat maple seeds. Neither of us had seen them there before, let alone in such large numbers. When you take the time to notice nature around you, even places you visit repeatedly can offer new experiences. Author photo

ture Observation doesn't follow a route, a clear trail will make it easier for you to wander without getting lost. At the end of your walk, you can use the trail markers to guide yourself back to your car.

It also helps if you can find a place away from traffic. That can be hard if your only local options are in a city, but do the best you can. Road noise will drown out nature sounds, and it may keep shyer species away.

More importantly, road noise will distract you. It will pull you away from the Deep Nature Observation mindset and back toward that fight-or-flight mode you want to escape.

I tend to emphasize forests when I think of Deep Nature Observation, largely because I'm a forester by training. If you live in a part of the world that has woods, look for publicly accessible ones to observe in. There's something about the presence of tall trees—especially conifers like pines and spruces—that soothes and relaxes us. Remember that shinrin yoku is "forest bathing," not "nature bathing."

Of course, if you don't live in an area with forests, time outdoors is still time well spent. You can practice Deep Nature Observation and get its health benefits without trees. Maybe you have prairie where you live, or stone canyons. Each of these settings offers a wealth of observation experiences, even if they aren't "forest" bathing per se.

Finally, find a place with water

if you can. As laid out in Wallace Nichols's excellent book *Blue Mind*, we have a strong affinity for water. The sights, sounds, and smells of water all relax us. Walking in a place with water will help you settle into that Deep Nature Observation mindset. As a bonus, many plants and wildlife live near water, so you're likely to see a greater diversity of species.

If you've spent a lot of time outdoors, you may already have ideas of places that meet the recommendations I just laid out. But if you're an indoors type, or if you live in a city, you might be struggling to think of places you can go.

Fortunately, there are a lot of lands open for public access—if you know where to look. Even in cities, there are typically parks and nature trails within walking distance.

Unfortunately, local parks and trails rarely advertise. You'll need to do some research online to find places near you. Here are a few resources I use:

- **Recreation.gov** – This website has information about U.S. government lands like national parks and forests. These lands are sometimes more suitable for vacations than regular trips, but they have some of the most breathtaking views in the country.

- **State and local park websites** – Use your favorite search engine and look up "[your state] state parks" or "[your city] parks and recreation." Odds are, you'll find a website for your city's or state's parks. You can then use that website to find where the parks are.

- **Alltrails.com** – There are several trail apps like AllTrails that can help you find not only public lands but long-distance routes like rail-trails. Always double-check the paths you find on these websites. Although these sites have gotten better, they will often have unofficial or unsanctioned trails on them.

Once you've found a place to visit, use technology to help you prepare

Places with water like streams, ponds, lakes, and oceans have a relaxing quality. Visiting places like these will help you get in the mindset for observing nature. Author photo

for observation. Two of my favorite websites (and smartphone apps) for this task are iNaturalist and eBird.

These two sites are citizen science projects. People use their smartphones to submit sightings of plants, birds, and other critters in the field. iNaturalist and eBird then display those sightings on worldwide, searchable maps.

What does that mean for you? If you're thinking about visiting a new park or forest, look that place up on iNaturalist and eBird. You'll get an idea of what species you're likely to see if you go there.

Knowing what to expect can hone your species identification practice ahead of time. Instead of learning hundreds of bird calls, for example, learn fifteen or twenty based on the birds eBird indicates you're most likely to hear.

TIME

Once you know where you want to go, how long do you need to stay there? How much time does it take to get the health benefits of Deep Nature Observation?

Forest bathing research shows it doesn't take much. As little as five minutes in nature is enough to significantly boost your mood.[1] Even if you can only get outside

TRY THIS — SPOT DIFFERENCES

Deep Nature Observation demands looking beyond the obvious. It asks us to become aware of the small details, subtle changes, and secret actions that make up the world around us.

We don't do this every day, so when we enter the woods, we need to consciously refocus our attention on our senses. One way to do that is to spot differences.

Next time you hit the trail, go with a partner. Before you start your walk, stand at the trailhead. Face each other six feet apart. Neither of you move.

Look at the other person and study them. Pay attention to every detail you can. What are they wearing? What's their expression? How have they done their hair? Have them study you the same way.

Now both of you shut your eyes. Keeping your eyes closed, each of you change one thing about your appearance. Maybe you'll change how you were standing, or the position of a hand. It doesn't matter what you choose.

Open your eyes. Try to spot the other person's change. Ask them to spot yours.

Repeat this process several times. When both you and your partner consistently spot each other's changes, you'll have prepared your mind for Deep Nature Observation. Now you're ready to explore.

for a few minutes a day—maybe on your lunch break at work, you can still see health benefits.

Of course, the more time you spend outside, the bigger and longer-lasting the benefits become. If you can manage an overnight, that delivers the most powerful health benefits. Recall from Chapter 2 that a three-day trip can boost immune function by more than 50 percent, and those benefits can last a month after the trip ends.

If I had to put the "ideal" timeframe on Deep Nature Observation, I would describe it this way. Get at least a few minutes outside every day. Take one morning or afternoon wandering each week, and do an overnight journey four times a year.

Now I'll be the first to admit that I don't meet this schedule. The pressures of life keep me away from the outdoors more than I would like—and frankly, more than is healthy.

And that's the point. Most of us are so far from this "ideal" time in nature schedule that any time outside is time well spent.

GEAR

What equipment do you need to practice Deep Nature Observation? This is a case where less is more. The more gear you bring, the greater the stress and distraction—the very two things you want to get away from.

Even so, there are some useful items to have even if you're just out for a stroll in the park. Most of these are classic outdoor gear and fall into the "common sense" category.

Wear sunscreen, sunglasses, and a hat to protect yourself from sunburns. For multi-hour explorations, carry water and snacks. If you're visiting somewhere new, bring a map.

Dress in layers. This is especially important for Deep Nature Observation. You'll be moving more slowly through nature than you may be used to. Temperatures that seem fine on a brisk walk can become

An overnight trip to the woods delivers the longest-lasting health benefits, so sprinkle in the occasional camping trip if and when you're able. Photo: Denys Nevozhai on Unsplash

frigid if you're sitting on the ground for an extended period observing a rotten log.

Comfort matters in Deep Nature Observation. If you're freezing or overheated, your fight-or-flight response will kick in. Your body will focus on its need to warm up or cool down, and you won't be able to focus as much on observing.

Something to record your observations is also a good idea. Many outdoor observers build a nature journal, a running record of what they find outside.

Nature journals typically combine drawings, writing, and photographs. They're useful for tracking your observations over time. You can look at how a place you visit changes with the seasons, or from year to year.

For more information on nature journaling, check out Chapter 11.

What about a camera? I'm an avid nature photographer, so I take my camera everywhere. I love taking pictures of landscapes, flowers, and especially birds. I've devoted all of Chapter 10 to improving your nature photography.

Cameras do have one drawback. They narrow your focus and make it harder to reach that state of soft fascination from the last chapter. You spend so much time narrowly searching for subjects to photograph that you miss the sounds, smells, and other sensory experiences nature has to offer.

My approach to the camera is to bring it but not plan to use it. I keep it in a belt pouch rather than around my neck. If I happen upon something I want to photograph, then I'll pull it out and take a picture. Otherwise I leave it in its case.

Marketers want you to think you need a ton of the latest, most expensive gear to get outside. You don't. To the contrary, spending time in nature is one of the most budget-friendly getaways you can have. Photo: Karson Chan on Unsplash.

If you bring a camera, splurge and get one with a strong built-in zoom or that can attach a telephoto lens. These lenses will help you photograph birds and other wildlife at a distance. Photo: Mogomotsi Makolo on Unsplash

That way I'm still free to explore nature with all my senses, free of the expectation of getting a photo.

TO PHONE OR NOT TO PHONE?

Now for the most controversial piece of outdoor gear: your smartphone. Do you bring it with you?

Few arguments get as heated in outdoor recreation as what to do with the smartphone. To some it's the bane of outdoor experience—an alluring siren that calls you back to the technological everyday world. To others it's the opposite—an at-your-fingertips field guide, map, compass, and emergency signal that enhances your time in nature.

I can see both sides of the debate. On the one hand, a smartphone offers remarkably useful abilities that, putting aside any impact on the outdoor experience, are smart from a safety perspective. In a worst-case scenario, a phone can literally save your life.

At the same time, that glowing screen and its tendency to suck you into it is exactly what you're hoping to escape when you engage in Deep Nature Observation. If you're staring into that screen—even to look up that weird bird you just saw—then you aren't observing nature.

Moreover, while we have to work hard to get ourselves out of our daily mindset and into Deep Nature Observation, the phone has the power to sway us instantly back to modern mode. It won't take long to respond to these texts. And while I'm at it I should check my e-mail… and my social media…

See what I mean? Even an innocuous glance at your phone for

A smartphone in nature can be distracting, but it can also enhance your experience if used carefully. Photo: Michał Bożek on Unsplash

something valuable to the nature experience can tempt you away from the outdoors and back into the go-go world you wanted to relax from.

For many—myself included—that temptation is too great. For that reason, I keep my phone turned off or in airplane mode when I head into nature.

But I do bring it, and as surprised as you may be to hear me say it, I recommend you bring yours too. Because for all the negative temptations the phone presents, its potential to enhance your experience is too great to ignore.

Safety is probably the biggest reason to bring your phone. If you get lost, you may be able to call or text for help. First responders can use the GPS in your phone to locate you quickly. You can also access maps and the compass in your phone to find out where you are and how to get back to your car.

But safety isn't the only reason. Certain apps are remarkably useful for Deep Nature Observation.

One of my favorites, Merlin, is a free app from the Cornell Lab of Ornithology. It's a bird identification app, and as the name suggests, its results can be magical.

Here's how it works. Download the free Merlin app on your phone. It goes outside with you, and you don't need coverage for it to work.

When you see a bird you want to identify, Merlin asks you a few simple questions about it, like,

"What size was the bird?" It shows silhouettes of common birds like robins, crows, and geese to make the questions easy to answer. Merlin then uses your answers to show possible birds you may have seen.

What makes Merlin really slick is that it uses more than just your answers. It also draws on that huge eBird database I told you about. It uses the GPS in your phone to figure out where you are, and then it looks at eBird to figure out which birds people have seen in that area. That narrows the list a lot, and it means you won't have to sort through birds that have never been seen in that place.

In all, Merlin gives you the best chance of any app I've found to make a correct bird ID in the field with the least possibility for error.

There are lots of other great identification apps like Merlin out there. Even generative AI tools like ChatGPT are getting into the game. These tools are surprisingly good at identifying trees and other plants with just a picture.

Adding to the fun, there are the myriad free astronomy apps out there. Take your pick on these. Most work the same way. Point your phone at the night sky, and the app uses your phone's GPS, compass, and accelerometer to know which stars you're facing. The app then displays those stars on the screen along with their names and any constellations they're part of. Some apps can also locate other celestial bodies like planets, satellites, and the International Space Station.

So as much as I would love to tell you to go into nature without any technology and observe the way our ancestors did, I can't bring myself to do it. I think the phone is worth the potential price.

And to be clear, you can avoid that price and still carry your phone. True, it takes some self-mastery to prevent the phone from pulling you out of your outdoor experience. But Deep Nature Observation is itself an exercise in self-mastery—a willingness to shed your modern life for a while in exchange for healing and connection. Master your phone, and it can help, rather than hinder, your journey.

Identifying birds like this scarlet tanager, as well as other plants and animals, has gotten a lot easier with smartphone apps, including generative AI. Photo: Mark Olsen on Unsplash

In the late 2000's, biologist Dr. David George Haskell did something that sounds crazy, even for someone who loves the outdoors like I do. He spent a year studying one square meter of forest—an area about the size of a kitchen table. Now that's Deep Nature Observation!

Haskell wrote a book about his experience called *The Forest Unseen: A Year's Watch in Nature*. It became a Pulitzer Prize finalist.

In *The Forest Unseen*, Haskell calls the area he studies "the mandala." The word comes from Hinduism and Buddhism, and it means "circle."

Mandalas are ritual symbols—small areas that represent the universe. In Haskell's case, by closely examining a few plants, insects, and fungi, he gains deeper understanding of the whole forest.

You don't need to spend a year studying one patch of earth, but applying a similar approach can improve your nature observation skills.

Choose an area you visit routinely that isn't likely to be disturbed. Measure a circle three feet across. This is your mandala.

As often as you're able, return to your mandala and see what's going on. Don't just glance at it as you walk past. Stop. Sit on a rock or fallen log. Lay on your stomach on the ground. Get up close and personal, inches from the action. Use a hand lens to enhance your view beyond what your naked eye can see. I have recommendations on buying and using hand lenses in the next chapter.

At first you'll probably be frustrated. You'll have thoughts like, "There's nothing here. Why am I lying on the ground? How did I let that crazy author talk me into this?"

Work through that frustration. Over time, you'll start to look more closely at your mandala. Instead of the entire circle, you'll notice individual plants. You may see snails climbing blades of grass.

From there the wonder begins. Are the snails on some plants but not on others? What makes them different?

Once you reach that point—the point of wonder—you'll understand why I find Deep Nature Observation so powerful for connecting with nature.

Repeatedly examining the same small natural area, like this bend in a stream, will force you to become more observant. It will also expose you to the remarkable diversity, dynamism, and interactivity that make up the world around you. Author photo

Chapter 4

SIGHT

The real voyage of discovery consists not of seeing new landscapes but in having new eyes.
— Marcel Proust

It's no surprise that I'm starting our sense-by-sense skill development with vision. As strong as our other senses are, we are visual creatures.

About 30 percent of the human brain's cerebral cortex—the part responsible for conscious thought—is devoted to visual processing. We have an entire brain lobe, the occipital lobe, devoted to it.

We also have the light-sensing hardware to put that processing power to use. You've probably heard that we have two types of cells in our eyes: rods and cones. Rods process low light and help us see in the dark. Cones help us see color.

But not all cone cells are the same. We actually have three kinds of cone cells, with each one responding to a different color: red, green, or blue.

When we see something, the cone cells send weaker or stronger signals to the brain based on how much of their assigned color they detect. Our brain puts that information together and comes up with a color for the object. Using various combinations of red, green, and blue, our brains can differentiate more than one million color shades.

Having three kinds of cone cells is rare among mammals like us. Most mammals only have two types of cones. As a result, many other mammals are red/green colorblind, unable to tell those colors apart.

Another visual advantage we have over many animals is our depth perception. With our eyes placed in the fronts of our heads, we can look out at a landscape and instantly identify which objects are closer and which are farther away.

Animals with their eyes on the sides of their heads, like horses, have very limited depth perception. They can see in a wider arc than we can, but they have trouble assessing distances.

For all the power our eyes possess, we don't use them anywhere near their potential. Usually that's because we're so focused on one thing that we ignore everything around it—like in the Invisible Gorilla Experiment. Other times it's the opposite. We're so distracted with our thoughts that we hardly see anything at all.

I want to cure you of both

Ever wonder why tigers are orange? Seems like they'd stick out among green plants (left). But it works because unlike us, most mammals are red/green colorblind. Viewed that way (right), the tiger blends in. Photo: Nick Fewings on Unsplash

conditions in this chapter. I want to give you techniques for seeing beyond the obvious. I want to help you find the color, beauty, and complexity hiding in plain sight—the invisible gorilla of nature standing in front of you beating its chest screaming for you to notice it. We'll also explore ways to enhance your vision to superhuman levels using optics like hand lenses and binoculars.

WIDE-ANGLE VISION

There's a scene in one of the *Lord of the Rings* movies that always confused me.

In *The Two Towers*, Aragorn, Legolas, and Gimli are chasing a pack of Uruk-hai. The monsters are miles ahead, so Aragorn asks Legolas for more information about what the bad guys are doing. "What do your Elf eyes see?" he asks.

Legolas stands on a small rise and stares. As though zooming in with a camera, he suddenly can see the detail of how the monsters are changing direction.

How does he do that? It puzzled me for a long time. How does he "zoom in" his vision like that?

Turns out, your eyes do the same thing, though not to such an extreme level. They scan the landscape. When they find something interesting, they focus on it.

Your vision has its strongest clarity in the center. So you turn your head toward the object of your attention. Your eyes adjust their focal distance to make the object clear. And your brain, which knows you want to pay attention to that object, subconsciously blurs the object's surroundings. That allows the brain to focus more processing power on the particular item you want to study.

All this happens instantly, instinctively, without you having to think about it.

Why am I writing a whole section about this? Because in the modern world, too often we miss the first step in this focusing process:

scanning the landscape. So much competes for our attention that our eyes never zoom back out.

I think that's why the movie scene confused me for so long. I'd been living my life zoomed in for so long that I forgot I even could zoom out.

It should come as no surprise that I'm using photography terms to describe what our eyes are doing. Like a camera, our eyes can adjust to different focal distances. To improve our nature observations, we must relearn how to zoom out—to supplement our everyday telephoto vision with wide-angle vision.

Soft fascination can help. When you let your attention direct itself, your eyes will naturally zoom out.

Once you're in that mindset, train yourself to focus not on the ground, but on the horizon. When we walk, too many of us have a habit of staring at or near our feet. What do you expect to see doing that? If you want a landscape view, you have to point your eyes at the landscape. Look up!

You also need to look out. I don't mean watch for danger, although in a natural sense, wide-angle vision is how prey animals spot predators. Because our vision is sharpest in the center, our eyes and brain naturally emphasize what's directly in front of us. We often ignore our peripheral vision entirely.

That's a mistake. Our peripheral vision is immensely powerful.

Did you know you have eyes in the back of your head? Not literally of course, but your peripheral vision can actually see past horizontal.

Think of it geometrically. A circle has 360 degrees. The half circle in front of you marks 180 degrees.

But your eyes can see more than that. They can see as far as 200 degrees—beyond "left" and "right."

Try this. Stretch your arms out to

In nature, practice looking at the horizon as your default mode of seeing. It will help you break your everyday habit of focusing on things really close to you. Photo: Mick Haupt on Unsplash

Our horizontal field of vision (shown here in blue) extends as far as 200 degrees. This strong peripheral vision gives us the ability to see objects that are slightly behind us. Author illustration

either side of you. Without turning your head, use your peripheral vision to look at your hands.

Now slowly move your arms back while keeping them straight. Your hands will clearly be behind you, but you'll still be able to see them.

Practice using your peripheral vision whenever you observe outside. We ignore it a lot in our daily lives. Like any sense, it dulls from lack of use.

As you experiment with wide-angle vision, you'll likely find that although you can see more, many objects appear fuzzy. That's normal. Wide-angle vision is meant for scanning the landscape and building awareness of a scene, not taking in detail.

Scanning the landscape this way does more than help you see a wider view. It also makes your eyes more sensitive to movement.

As visual animals, we key in on movement. Movement indicates another animal. In ancient times, it meant possible food from prey or danger from predators.

If you want to see more wildlife, wide-angle vision is essential. It's in this wide, unfocused view that our brain is most attuned to movement.

When you do notice movement, your eyes will instinctively zoom in to focus on it. Let them. Wide-angle vision takes a lot of effort, both for the eyes and for the brain to process all that information. Switching back and forth from zoomed in to zoomed out will reduce eye strain and maintain interest.

If you want to expand your wide-angle vision even more, try changing your vantage point by getting a tree stand.

If you're a hunter, you've probably used a tree stand. But you don't need a weapon to sit in one. Tree stands are excellent for seeing more of the

TRY THIS — SEE THROUGH NOVEMBER DRAB

Ah, November. Is there a worse month for exploring nature? Autumn leaves have dropped. Birds have flown south. Yet neither has winter lain its white snowpack, nor the songs of owls and chickadees begun. What a drab, boring, waste of a month.

Or is it? November may lack the showy beauty of other months, but that makes it the perfect time to practice your visual observation. November forces you to look beyond the obvious for nature's more subtle beauties. That experience will carry with you into other months and make them even more vibrant.

But what is there to see in November, really? Wildflowers for one. Even after several frosts, you can still find some late bloomers hanging on. Asters give a spark of white. Wild geraniums provide a pale purple.

Witch hazel and goldenrod can turn fields, roadsides, and thickets lemon-yellow. Witch hazel in particular is a fun flower to study up close. Each flower is made up of four narrow, half- to three-quarter-inch long petals. They also have a spicy fragrance, so give them a sniff when you find them.

November is also a time of frosts. One late fall morning, hoarfrost descended on my neighborhood. Old English defines hoarfrost as frost that resembles "an old man's beard." When I peered closely at the leaves clinging to a few hardy plants, I was amazed at the long, white crystals spreading along the leaf margins. That day, I understood how this beautiful phenomenon got its name. Author Photo

More commonly used for hunting, a tree stand can give you a new vantage point for observations by getting you above the visual attention of many animals. Photo: Melissa Gonzalez, U.S. Fish and Wildlife Service

landscape and more wildlife. By getting up high, you can see more of the woods around you. Stands also get you above the visual attention areas of many animals, so they'll be less likely to notice you and potentially come closer.

Finally, tree stands more or less force you to sit still or risk falling out of them. By sitting still, animals are again less likely to spot you. Remember, just as you're looking for signs of movement, so are they. Only when they see movement, their response will be to run in the other direction.

THREE-DIMENSIONAL VISION

As I mentioned above, we have superb depth perception. Suppose we stood together in a field, and I pointed out two trees in that field some distance away. At a glance, you could tell which tree was closer to us. You would do this instantly and subconsciously. It's simply part of our impressive eyesight and visual processing.

As powerful as this natural ability is, it has limits on its own. Consider those two trees again. Even though trees are obviously three-dimensional, our brain often interprets them as flat.

Why? It has to do with our eyes' focal distance.

Let's do an experiment. Hold this book straight out in front of you so you can see both the book and the wall behind it at the same time. Are both in focus? No. The book will be in focus, and the wall will be blurry. You can change your attention and focus on the wall, but then the book will be blurry.

A similar situation happens in nature. When you look at a tree, your eyes focus on the parts of it that are closest to you. Everything deeper in goes blurry. This makes the plant appear as a flat, impenetrable blob.

But just as you can consciously change your focus from the book to the wall, you can change your focus from the outside of the tree to the inside.

Unlike our usual binocular vision, this shift takes effort. The brain instinctively focuses on what's closest to us. It assumes closer objects are more important.

This makes sense biologically. The

lion that's ten feet away is a bigger danger than the one that's a hundred feet away.

The point, though, is that we can override this natural inclination. When we do, we gain a remarkable nature observation power: the ability to literally see through objects.

Let's go back to the tree. It appears as a solid mass, but it isn't. Even when the tree has all its leaves, there are a lot of blank spaces between them—spaces we can see through.

Changing your focus this way is essential for spotting wildlife. It's immensely frustrating to hear a bird sing, look in its direction, and see only the green blob of a tree. You know the bird is there, but you can't see it.

Birds in trees rarely perch on the end of a branch. Instead, they sit farther in. They're relying on this flaw in our—and predators'—vision

to hide themselves.

Other wildlife do this too. Deer will often take cover behind a shrub. They may be plainly visible, but you won't see them because your eyes focus on the shrub and not what's behind it.

When in the woods, train your eyes to look past the closest edge of plants. Even when you don't suspect an animal is hiding, deliberately change your attention so the branches behind the first visible row come into focus.

Birdwatching is my favorite way to practice three-dimensional vision. Use the listening skills in the next chapter to find a bird, then look into the tree or shrub it's hiding in. Shift your focus past the plant's outer leaves, and you may find the bird singing.

The more you practice three-dimensional vision, the faster you'll

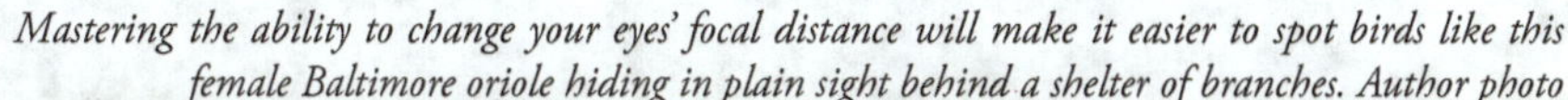

Mastering the ability to change your eyes' focal distance will make it easier to spot birds like this female Baltimore oriole hiding in plain sight behind a shelter of branches. Author photo

TRY THIS — WATCH A METEOR SHOWER

A good way to practice both your night vision and wide-angle vision is to watch a meteor shower. You'll need dark-adjusted eyes to see meteors, and you'll need wide-angle vision to cover as much of the sky as possible.

Meteors, often referred to as shooting stars, aren't really stars. They're pieces of dust or rock from space that hit our atmosphere. When they do, they burn with extreme heat, which causes them to glow and become visible.

Perhaps the best known and most reliable meteor shower is the Perseid Meteor Shower. It happens annually from mid-July to late August, with the peak usually around August 12 or 13. It's visible throughout the northern hemisphere and happens in the same area of the sky as the constellation Perseus. Not sure where that is? A stargazing app can point you in the right direction. Minimize use of it, though, to preserve your night vision.

The best times to view meteors are late at night, between midnight and dawn. After midnight, the part of the Earth where you are has turned into the direct path of the dust that forms the meteor shower. That means more meteors to spot.

To see meteors, get away from city lights and out into the country. Choose a clear night with as little moon as possible. Bring layers of clothing, even though it's summer. You'll be sitting or lying still for a long time, so you may get chilly otherwise.

As dramatic as the name "meteor shower" sounds, it's not really a rain of meteors. They come slowly. Plan to stay out for at least half an hour. Bring a beach chair or yoga mat you can lie down on. That will make extended sky viewing more comfortable.

You don't need a telescope or binoculars to watch a meteor shower. Stick with your eyes. They'll give you the widest view of the sky. Don't focus on one area either. Instead, let your eyes wander. Relaxed eyes will have an easier time spotting meteors.

Meteor showers give you a cosmic lightshow, but only if you get away from city lights. Photo: Pixabay

get. Eventually, when you walk in the woods, you'll instinctively look not at a tree, but through it. At that point you'll be amazed just how much more wildlife has been around you all this time that you never noticed before.

ENHANCE YOUR NIGHT VISION

While humans have amazing vision in good light, we aren't as well equipped at night. The same cone cells that let us see more than a million shades of color simply don't work well without a lot of light.

When the sun goes down, we rely on our rod cells. Rods don't see color, but they can work in lower light levels. The trade-off is that because we have cone-dominated eyes, we lack the night vision acuity of animals with rod-dominated eyes like cats.

That said, we have plenty of rod cells, and our night vision is better than we give ourselves credit for. It's certainly good enough to let us observe nature after dark, but because of its limitations, we need to give our eyes every advantage possible.

Now when I talk about enhancing your night vision, the first thing you may jump to is a flashlight. Want to see more at night? Add more light!

But a flashlight or headlamp can actually cause the opposite and make you see less. First of all, the bright light will scare wildlife and make them move away. More importantly, the light beam will limit your own range of sight to the narrow area the

Red lights don't affect our night vision as much, so they're a good option when stargazing. Photo: William Pedro, National Park Service

light illuminates. There goes your wide-angle vision.

That said, it's still worth carrying a flashlight when you do nighttime observations. It's useful if you need to consult a map or in emergency situations.

If you use a flashlight for observation, a red-tinted one is your best option. You can DIY this by using a rubber band to attach red plastic wrap or tissue paper over your flashlight lens. You can also buy red flashlight bulbs, and some flashlights even come with a "red light" setting.

Red-tinted flashlights work for outdoor observation because if you recall, most mammals are red/green colorblind. They're missing the cone cells that pick up red light. That means if you shine a red flashlight on them, they won't react to it as

A full moon is surprisingly bright and can help your nighttime observations. It will wreck your stargazing though by blotting out many dimmer stars. If you mainly want to observe the night sky, choose nights with little to no moon. Photo: Brice Cooper on Unsplash

strongly as if you used the bare light. A red flashlight also has the advantage of being easier on your night vision than pure white light.

The best option, though, is to avoid the flashlight altogether. Instead, do your nighttime observations on a night with a clear sky and a full moon. The full moon reflects a good amount of sunlight down onto Earth, so you can see surprisingly well by it.

To enhance your night vision further, use patience. Your eyes need a long time to adjust to the dark. Those light-sensitive rod cells get overwhelmed by the normal amount of light we're exposed to. They need to rest before they can do their best night vision work. Allow yourself at least half an hour and even up to an hour to see the lowest level of light possible.

At all times while doing night vision observation, avoid looking at any light source. Don't stare directly at the moon. If you come upon other people using flashlights, ask them to turn them off until they pass you. If they won't do that, avoid looking at the beams as best you can. Even a second or two of bright light exposure will overwhelm your rod cells. That means another half-hour wait before your night vision is ready again.

Put that wide-angle vision to use. Your eyes have more light-sensitive rod cells along the edges than in the center. That means you have the best night vision not directly in front of you but in your peripheral vision. When you notice an object at night that you want to focus on, avoid the natural inclination to center your vision on it. Instead, turn your head slightly away from it and look using the sides of your eyes.

You can further energize your rod cells by keeping your eyes moving. Don't focus on one object for long. Sweep the landscape. That will keep your eyes sensitive and alert. Frequent blinking helps maintain this sensitivity as well.

You can also try a gentle eye massage. Close your eyes, then apply light pressure on them with the fleshy part of your hand just below the thumb. Do this for about five seconds, then wait another ten or fifteen seconds before opening your eyes again.

Location will also influence your night vision. For stargazing, pick an open area. If you want to hike, choose a trail with a lot of light-colored rocks like limestone nearby. The rocks will reflect more light and make the trail easier to navigate. For the best chance to spot nocturnal animals, head into a forest so your eyes can get as deep into night vision as possible.

Diet can affect your night vision too. Foods with a lot of vitamin A are especially good. The body uses vitamin A to make the light-absorbing substance in the eyes. Foods like carrots, broccoli, and fish are all high in vitamin A. Shellfish, tomatoes, and blueberries are also solid options.

Finally, when doing nighttime observations, keep a few safety pointers in mind. For your first walk, pick a trail you know well. It will feel more familiar and less scary at night.

Slow your pace even more than you do for daytime observations. You don't want to miss an exposed root and twist an ankle.

Bring layers of clothes, because the temperature can drop a lot at night. Make sure you have a cell phone for emergencies, and tell someone where you'll be going.

Most importantly, go with a friend or group. A lot of Deep Nature Observation assumes you're going solo, because it's easier to see wildlife if you don't have a big group talking and clomping through nature. With after-dark hikes, though, bringing a buddy will help you feel safer. Most public lands are extremely safe, but having a partner will, if nothing else, ease your mind when you hear an unexpected twig snap.

WILDLIFE TRACKS AND OTHER SIGNS

Many animals flee when they sense humans nearby. For that reason, you may not see much wildlife when you go for walks in nature. A more reliable method of knowing which animals use your local park or forest is to look for the signs they leave behind, like tracks.

Tracks can tell you a lot about animals. Apart from revealing which critters passed by, tracks can reveal an animal's size (by how large the

It takes a long time for rod cells in your eyes to reach peak performance. Even a couple seconds of light exposure can wreck your night vision for half an hour. Photo: Oliver Guhr on Unsplash

track is), speed (by how far apart the tracks are), and how recently it visited (by how wet or dry the track is).

If you live in an area that gets snow, winter is an ideal time to see animal tracks. My favorite time to look for tracks is the day after a small snowfall—the kind where you get three inches or less. Those conditions are ideal for animals to leave tracks, and you'll likely surprise yourself with how many you spot.

Tracks aren't the only wildlife sign. Many animals have unique signs to signal their presence. Bears will stand on their hind legs and rub or claw trees to show other bears how big they are. Male deer accomplish the same task by scraping their antlers against small trees.

Bite marks are another sign. In this case, they can help you figure out what's been eating your garden. Deer will leave a ragged edge, because they don't have upper incisors. By contrast, rabbits will leave a clean cut, almost like you cut the plant with pruning shears.

Another telling wildlife sign is scat, and yes, that means poo. Every animal does it.

More valuable for you as someone exploring nature, every animal does it in a different way based on its size, diet, and digestive system. If you can stomach the learning process, scat can tell you not just what animal left it, but how long ago and whether that critter is in good health.

PRESERVE ANIMAL TRACKS

Once you've found some animal tracks, preserving them can be as easy as taking a picture with your phone. But you can go further

The moisture in a track can give you a sense of how recently an animal passed through an area. The black bear that made this fresh track isn't too far away. Author photo

than that and bring back a physical memento of wildlife tracks you find by using plaster of paris.

Get an empty 2-liter soda bottle. Cut the top off so you have a straight cylinder. Now cut off another ring about two inches wide.

Head outside and look for an area with wet ground. Wet ground will preserve tracks better than dry dirt or snow. Streambanks, river edges, and other spots near water are good places to search. You want a deep track pressed well into the ground so the plaster has something to mold into.

When you find a track you want to preserve, lay your soda bottle ring around the track. Press the ring into the ground a little so it forms a kind of plastic wall surrounding the track. Remove any leaves, stones, twigs, or other debris from the circle.

Now you'll need plaster of paris. Bring along the plaster, a large tin can, and a bottle of water. Pour some water and plaster into the can. Follow the plaster directions to know how much water and plaster to add.

Stir the water and plaster slowly with a spoon or wooden mixing stick until the consistency becomes like pancake batter. Do your best not to get air bubbles in the mix.

Remove the spoon. Gently tap the bottom of the can on a rock to remove any air bubbles. Keep tapping until any bubbles stop.

With your plaster mixed, pour it into your circle. To avoid damaging the track, pour only along the

Winter is a great time to look for wildlife tracks. Choose a day right after a light snow for the best results. Author photo

outside of the ring, not in the track itself. Let the plaster naturally run down into the track on its own.

Pour enough plaster so it almost fills to the top of your soda bottle ring wall. It will take an hour to harden, so go for a walk and come back.

To remove your track, you need to be careful. The plaster will still be soft, and it will crack if you just yank it from the ground. Instead, dig a ditch around your soda bottle ring. Slowly work your way in under the track, pulling away mud. When about half the ring is suspended in midair, try carefully lifting it by pushing up from the now-exposed bottom. If you feel any resistance, stop and dig away more mud.

When the ring lifts gently away, it's not time to celebrate. The plaster

Deep tracks in soft mud (left) will preserve better than shallow ones in dry dirt (right). Author photos

is still fragile and can break easily during transport. Wrap it in some newspaper to help it survive the journey home.

Back indoors, put your plaster cast somewhere it won't be disturbed for at least two days. You'll know when the plaster is really dry because it will feel cool to the touch.

The result of this work is what's called a "negative" cast. Where the original track formed an imprint, your plaster cast will show a raised print (because you filled in the hole the track created). You can stop here if you want, or you can use that negative cast to create a "positive" one—a cast that is an imprint just like the original track.

To make a positive cast, first get an empty milk carton (not the plastic kind, but the waxed cardboard type). Cut off the bottom so you have a piece with the bottom of the carton and walls about three inches high. This will be your mold.

Fill the mold with plaster of paris and let it start to set. While you wait, take some vegetable shortening and rub it gently on your original negative cast from outside.

As soon as the plaster mix starts to harden, take your negative cast and carefully make an impression in the hardening plaster. The timing is crucial. Too early, and the plaster will fill in on itself and not form a track. Too late, and the drying plaster will crack from the pressure of you pushing down on it with your negative cast. This step takes some trial and error, but eventually you'll get a feel for the consistency you need to get a good positive cast.

Once you've made your imprint, remove your negative cast and gently wipe it clean. Set your positive cast in a place where it won't be disturbed for a couple days. When it's cool to the touch, you'll have a finished imprint that looks identical to the track you saw outside.

BEYOND THE NAKED EYE PART 1: HAND LENSES

Our eyes are impressive, but they

have limits. They're designed for sweeping the savanna for lions, not studying individual grass blades.

Unfortunately, much of nature happens at that tiny scale. To observe it, we need to enhance our vision beyond its natural capabilities. A hand lens provides a superb way to do that.

Hand lenses are small magnifying glasses. Jewelers use them to study precious stones, but you can use them to study the natural world. They're cheap to buy, straightforward to use, and reveal details you could never see otherwise.

Because they're inexpensive, get a couple different strengths to give you flexibility. You can get a simple 3x or 5x hand lens for less than $10. Both work well for basic magnification. If you want to go closer in, pick up a 10x magnifier, which is also common and inexpensive.

Don't bother going higher than 10x magnification. More magnification might sound better, but it's not. Above 10x, hand lenses become impractical to use outside. You have to hold these lenses extremely close to both your eye and the object you're studying—not an easy task in nature.

You could spend more money on professional lenses, but outdoor use is hard on hand lenses. Opt for cheap ones instead and just replace them when they get scratched or broken.

That said, it's worth spending a few extra dollars to get glass lenses rather than plastic ones. Plastic lenses get scratched and blurry more easily than glass ones do, so they don't hold up outside.

I also recommend against buying magnifiers that come with multiple lenses in sequence. In theory this

Hand lenses are cheap, simple ways to reveal nature's complexity. Photo: National Park Service

Now that you know how to use hand lenses, let's put them to work. In an Egg-Carton Observation, you'll study the details of something small. The only rule? Your subject has to be small enough to fit inside one of the divots in an egg carton. Flowers, leaves, mushrooms, and lichens are all good examples.

The aim with an Egg-Carton Observation is to notice as much as you can about something tiny. To do this, bring colored pencils and your nature journal outside with you.

When you do your observation, start with a sketch. Artistic quality doesn't matter. Just do your best. Focus on capturing every detail.

Use your hand lenses to maximize what you can see. Make your drawing larger than life so you can illustrate the details you can't see without the help of magnification.

Next, write about the object. Continue to add as much detail as possible. You might draw arrows to identify certain features.

Finally, write freehand about the object's role in its environment. Where did you find it? What is it part of? What does it do? Write down the species if you know it, but don't worry if you can't identify it.

The more of these observations you do, the better tuned your vision will become to nature's detail. Eventually, even when you don't pull out your hand lens, your eyes will pick up more of the small features and complexities of everyday objects you otherwise would have missed.

Individual flowers make good subjects for Egg-Carton Observations. They're small, intricate, and—important for this activity—stationary. Author photo

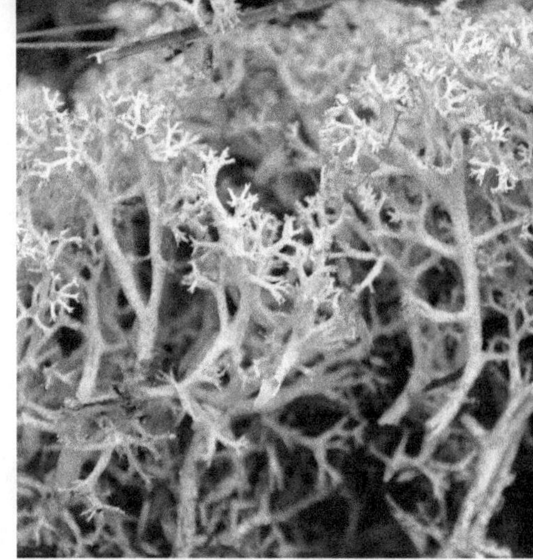

To the naked eye, lichens appear basic and unadorned. But viewed up close, they come in an astounding variety of colors and shapes. Studying lichens and other objects through magnification will give you a deeper understanding and appreciation of nature's complexity. Photos: U.S. Fish and Wildlife Service

setup is great, because by using different lens combinations, you get several magnifications with one piece of equipment.

But theory isn't practice. In my experience, these multi-lens magnifiers are hard to use and distort images more than single lenses do. Considering how cheap decent hand lenses have become, you're better off just buying two lenses of different magnifications.

Some magnifiers come with an LED to light up your object. It isn't required, but it's handy. If you're observing objects in the woods, for example, you're likely to be in heavy shade. The extra light from the LED will let you see deeper detail than you could otherwise.

Hand lenses take practice to use. To produce a clear image, the lens needs to be a set distance from both your eye and whatever you're studying.

What those distances are will vary depending on the lens you buy and its magnification. When you get a new lens, experiment with it in your home or backyard. Practice until your muscle memory intuitively puts you, the lens, and the object you're observing in the right spots to get a clear image.

Most people starting out with hand lenses hold them too far away from their eye. With higher magnifications, you'll get the best image by holding the lens as close to your eye as possible and then adjusting your distance to the object you want to observe.

As a final tip, when you get your hand lens, tie a colorful cord to it. I suggest hot pink. Hand lenses are small. At some point you will set your lens on the ground or drop it while walking. If you have that bright cord attached to it, your odds of finding it again are a lot higher.

BEYOND THE NAKED EYE PART 2: BINOCULARS

Hand lenses work great for stationary objects, but they're of little value for wildlife. To observe birds, deer, and other animals at a safe distance, swap the hand lens for binoculars or a spotting scope.

Let's start with binoculars. Decent binoculars are must-have equipment if you want to see more wildlife, especially birds. They're also useful for studying other objects you can't get close to, like buds or leaves way up in the canopy.

Unfortunately, there are so many binocular options that it's hard to know what to look for. Worse, they range in price from less than $100 to more than $2,000. What's worth buying, what's overpriced, and what's junk?

When choosing binoculars, you'll see that every pair has two numbers in a pattern like 7x42, 6x30, 10x50, etc. You read these numbers by saying, for example, "seven by forty-two."

The first number is the magnification. A "7" set of binoculars enlarges an image seven times.

As with hand lenses, higher magnification isn't necessarily better. If you get something too high, you'll never see anything. Your field of vision will be so small that fast-moving birds will be gone before you find them in your binoculars.

To balance magnification with usability, go for a magnification between six and eight. My binoculars have 8x magnification, and I really enjoy them.

The second number describes the size of the lens at the fat end of the binoculars. The bigger the number, the larger the lens. Larger lenses let in more light, so they show more detail and work better in low-light conditions like dawn and dusk.

The trade-off is that big lenses are bulky, which can make them impractical to carry all day. Small binoculars are more portable, but they need bright conditions to work well.

As with magnification, aim for a middle-of-the-road second number. Something between 35 and 45 seems to be the sweet spot. My binoculars are 42. They're easy to carry, and I've never had issues seeing birds even on dawn treks.

Pro tip: If you're buying binoculars for a child, most so-called "kid's binoculars" are terrible. Get them even a basic set of adult binoculars. Their experience will be a lot better. Photo: Jen Theodore on Unsplash

Older binoculars like my grandfather's (left) have the big lenses spaced farther apart than the eye lenses. By contrast, most modern binoculars (right) have the lenses in straight tubes. Straight tubes deliver better image quality, so look for them when buying binoculars. Author photos

Aside from numbers, certain features will improve your viewing experience. Look for binoculars that have one focusing knob for both tubes rather than separate ones. Two knobs take too long to adjust and are therefore impractical. Also look for waterproof binoculars, which are less likely to fog up.

If you wear glasses, ensure your binoculars have adjustable eye cups to accommodate them. Most decent modern binoculars have these.

Putting all this together, you might think the only way to get good binoculars is to drop a lot of money. That isn't the case. High-end binoculars distinguish themselves not in these core features, but in extras like better-quality lenses, anti-reflective coatings, and nitrogen purging (don't ask).

Do these features improve the viewing experience? I guess. Are they worth spending $2,000? Not in my opinion. You can get all the core features I described above in binoculars that cost less than $200.

Finally, I recommend also buying a binocular harness. It costs about $20 and will literally save your neck. Instead of hanging your binoculars around your neck by the neck strap, the harness goes over both shoulders and wraps across your back. The harness holds your binoculars in front of you for easy access. More importantly, it distributes their weight across your torso to avoid straining your neck.

BEYOND THE NAKED EYE PART 3: SPOTTING SCOPES

If you want even more magnification power, rather than binoculars, get a spotting scope. If you're not familiar with them, they're basically small telescopes. They're typically mounted on a tripod and used for stationary viewing rather than mobile observations.

Spotting scopes are useful when you can't get close enough to an animal to see it well even with binoculars. They're particularly good for waterfowl and shorebirds, as these birds may be far out on a lake or ocean and physically impossible to approach.

Spotting scopes are also useful at closer distances for seeing greater detail than you could otherwise. The greater magnification allows you to see feather patterns in far more intricacy than you could through binoculars.

Unlike binoculars, which have fixed magnification, many spotting scopes can change magnification. Some have interchangeable eyepieces, while others have one adjustable eyepiece.

An adjustable eyepiece might sound great, because you don't need to swap lenses. Unfortunately, adjustable eyepieces let in less light compared with fixed magnification ones at the same power. That means the image won't be as clear, particularly if you're observing in low light at dawn or dusk.

If you're willing to spend more, high-quality zoom lenses do exist that minimize this loss and deliver results almost as crisp as fixed magnification ones. For those with extra cash, it's worth splurging on a high-quality zoom lens to reduce the amount of time between finding a bird at low power and getting a detailed look at high magnification.

As for what magnification to use, spotting scopes range from around 15-60x, compared with 6-8x for binoculars. Whether using fixed or zoom eyepieces, it's best to start with a low-power magnification so you have the widest field of view

Spotting scopes are best used from a stationary location such as a wildlife blind or designated viewing area. Photo: Pablò on Unsplash

possible. Once you've centered your subject in the scope, switch to higher magnification for more detail.

For general wildlife watching, including most birding, you won't need anything larger than 30x. Higher magnifications can have so much distortion from heat and atmospheric effects that they won't give clear images unless they have extremely high quality (and expensive) optics.

Similar to binoculars, spotting scopes are advertised with a number that indicates the size of the lens at the far end in millimeters, usually between 50 and 100 millimeters. Also like binoculars, the size of that lens determines the scope's light-gathering capacity. A bigger number lets in more light and makes the scope more useful in low-light situations, but it also means the scope will be heavier and less portable.

If you need to hike a long way to your destination, a lighter scope will make a big difference. By contrast, if you plan to do a lot of your spotting at areas close to a parking spot (like, say, a lake or beach), you can go heavier with no real loss.

And it is worth getting that larger size if you can. A 60-millimeter far-end lens is considered the absolute minimum for good viewing. If you want to use your scope to take pictures (see Chapter 10), you'll need a lens of at least 85 millimeters.

Also like binoculars, look for scope models that are waterproof and fogproof. Moisture inside your scope is one of the worst things that

Spotting scopes are excellent for waterfowl observation, since you often can't get physically close enough even for binoculars. Author photo

can happen to it. Considering how expensive scopes are, you don't want to ruin yours because you got caught in a thunderstorm.

As for shape, look for scopes that have a 45-degree angled eyepiece. This style is more comfortable to look in and works particularly well when birding in a group. You can set the tripod at one height and multiple people will be able to look through it. With a straight-line setup, there will be a lot more stooping and stretching.

Get a good, sturdy, adjustable tripod to pair with your scope. A weak tripod won't hold steady, especially in windy conditions like at the beach. The result will be blurry images. Make sure the tripod can adjust for uneven ground quickly without a lot of fuss.

If you wear glasses, look for a spotting scope with an "eye relief" of 12 to 15 millimeters. Eye relief measures how far back from the eyepiece the image gets its sharpest clarity. Eyeglass wearers need a longer eye relief distance to compensate for the increased distance between their eyes and the eyepiece.

Another number worth looking at is the "field of view," commonly reported either in degrees or in feet at 1,000 yards. A wider field of view will let you see more at any given magnification. It's especially useful if you want to track moving objects, say that hawk soaring overhead or the flock of snow geese that just took off.

Spotting scopes adjust their focus in a couple ways. Some have a collar you rotate, similar to a manual-focusing camera lens. Others have a knob. The collar setup is faster but less precise. Try a couple models and see which method you prefer.

Spotting scopes are a specialized piece of nature observation equipment. With binoculars, I concluded that you can get a good pair for relatively little money. But if you're considering a spotting scope, it's worth getting a high-quality model.

Cut-price scopes that cost a few hundred dollars simply won't give you a good, crisp image.

Rather than waste your money, save up the $1,000 to $2,000 it takes to get a good midrange scope with high-quality optics and an excellent zoom lens. If you care for it, it will be the only one you ever buy.

Since spotting scopes are such a major purchase, always try before you buy. Don't buy your scope online, at least not without using the one you want first.

Start by visiting outdoor suppliers or a specialized birding store if one exists in your area. They'll usually let you test a few models.

If you have birding friends who already have scopes, go with them on some walks and try their scopes. Find out what you like and don't like.

Finally, seek out local birding festivals. Birders and manufacturers will often bring scopes to these events for attendees to try. The more scopes you experiment with, the more confident you'll be when you buy your own.

Spotting scopes also work for observing large animals, like bison, that would be dangerous to approach. Photo: Brian Miller on Unsplash

HEARING

I value my garden more for being full of blackbirds than of cherries, and very frankly give them fruit for their songs.
— Joseph Addison

Your alarm blares and forces you from sleep. Already the traffic honks and wails. You climb into the shower, where the water hisses down on you. By the time you get out, the people upstairs are up and banging around too. You wake the kids, and they start yelling even before their eyes open. You turn on the TV while you eat breakfast, but you can't hear it over everything else.

On your way to work, you crank the stereo to drown out the traffic. When you arrive, everyone gossips around the coffeepot. Between conversations, the air conditioner grinds white noise.

When the work day ends, it's back to horns, sirens, and tire squeals. In the evening, the kids shout so loud the neighbors complain. When everyone else goes to bed, you finally lull yourself to sleep with the TV's drone.

Sound bombards us every waking minute, every single day. If you live in a city, noise can seem inescapable. The only way to avoid it is to cover it up with something louder.

As noisy as our lives are, we often don't realize how constant that barrage is. We tune it out as background, learn to ignore it. But it's still there, and it's doing us harm.

Sound volume is measured in decibels, and continued exposure to anything louder than 85 decibels can cause hearing loss. In some large cities, people routinely experience that amount.

Even if the sound isn't that loud, constant noise harms us in other ways. It increases blood pressure, interferes with concentration, worsens sleep, and can cause forgetfulness.

It also exhausts our ears. Like any other body part, hearing tires from constant stimulation. That's why we tune out all that noise. Our ears are so tired they lose the ability to listen.

That loss hinders our ability to truly hear nature. We often describe nature as silent, but it isn't. Birds sing. Streams burble. Leaves rustle. Unlike human-made sounds, these natural sounds improve our health. Researchers from Brighton and Sussex Medical School in the

U.K. compared how people respond to natural and human-made sounds. Where human-made sounds made participants feel stressed, natural sounds relaxed them and let them perform better on cognitive tasks.[1]

You can hear some natural sounds just by entering a park or forest, but the subtler ones—the harmonies of plants, animals, and water mixing together—can't be heard with urban ears. To truly take in nature's orchestra and absorb its healing power, you must first consciously turn off your mental hearing block.

LISTEN TO THE "SILENCE"

The mental hearing block is hard to break. It's the brain's way of protecting itself from going crazy at the cacophony of urban life.

You need a big jolt to reset that block. The best jolt I've found is to make the brain experience something it believes no longer exists: silence.

Some years back, I accompanied fifteen high schoolers from the Bronx on a field trip to the Catskill Mountains. We hiked deep into the forest, more than a mile from the nearest road.

At the farthest point from civilization, our guide had the kids spread out around the woods. She asked them to close their eyes and

Residents of large cities routinely experience high levels of noise. This map of Philadelphia shows the background sound level in the city in decibels, or dB. Areas close to highways and airports are especially bad. Data source: U.S. Department of Transportation Noise Map

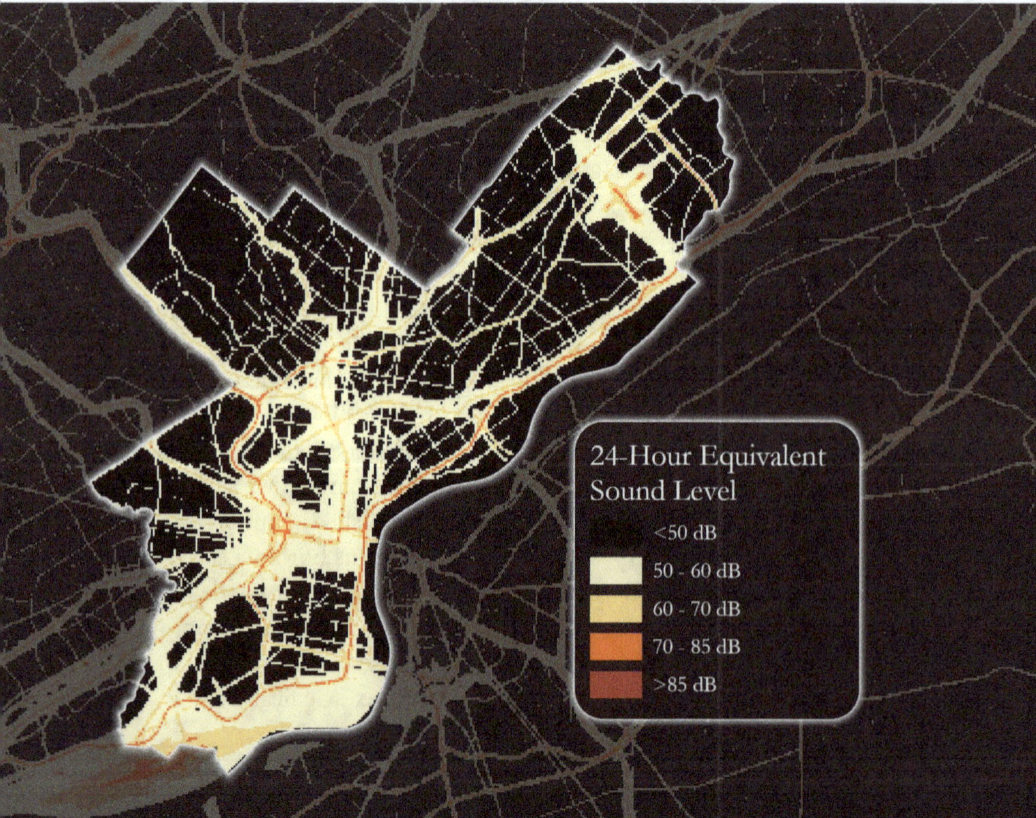

be silent for one minute.

That's all. One minute.

They couldn't do it.

The kids tried five times. Someone always laughed, coughed, or spoke.

When we got back to the bus, we talked with the group about their hike. Every student said the most impactful part was that failed attempt at silence. These inner city kids had grown up knowing only the thrum of urban life. The idea of silence was so foreign to them that they couldn't handle it. They had to interrupt it.

To truly listen to nature, you'll need to do better than those kids did. Head to the woods and go as far back on a trail as you feel comfortable going. Get as far from roads and other hikers as possible.

Now close your eyes and listen to nothing at all. Don't speak. Don't cough. Don't laugh. Can you make it one minute? It sounds easy, but you'll be surprised how difficult it is.

Keep that silence going as long as you can. Eventually your brain will stop blocking out sound and instead seek it. That's why your first instinct will be to make noise.

Move past that instinct. Once you do, your brain will switch to listening mode. It will search for sounds in the environment. You'll gradually find that the "silence" around you isn't silent at all. When you reach that realization, you'll know you've broken through your sensory numbness and are ready for deep listening.

For a true silence reset, go outside in winter on a calm day when there's snow on the ground. Fewer animals sing or call during winter, and snow muffles sound. Your brain will search even harder to find sound, and that effort will hone your nature listening. Author photo

THREE-DIMENSIONAL LISTENING

In the last chapter, we discussed three-dimensional vision: the ability to change your eyes' focal distance to look through an object and see the animal hiding inside it. You can do something similar with hearing. With practice, you can learn not just where a sound is coming from but how far away that sound is.

This three-dimensional listening is essential to birding in particular, but it's handy for anyone looking to deepen their outdoor experience.

Three-dimensional listening is important for Deep Nature Observation, because you'll often hear a sound before you see the creature making it. The faster you can pinpoint a sound's location, the better chance you have of catching the animal before it leaves. Three-dimensional listening helped me find this male common yellowthroat quickly enough to photograph him singing his "wichity-wichity-witch" song. Author photo

Three-dimensional listening is trickier than three-dimensional vision. Our anatomy isn't set up as well for it.

With vision, our eyes can shift focus quickly, and they're ideally positioned for depth perception. By contrast, our ears are fixed on the sides of our heads. That puts us at a disadvantage compared with some other mammals.

Think of a deer. It has huge, dish-like ears that stick up, swivel in any direction, and move independent of one another. That flexibility makes it easier for them to pinpoint a sound's location.

You can't give yourself swivel ears, but you can do something similar using your hands and body.

Suppose you hear a faint bird call in the distance. You have an idea of where it's coming from, but it's too quiet to tell what it is.

Face the sound and cup your ears from behind with your hands. Keep your fingers extended and together. Using your thumb and index finger, gently push your ears forward.

The slight change in ear shape, combined with your extended other fingers, will funnel more of those distant sound waves to your ears. That will make the sound louder.

What if you can't tell where that call is coming from? Recall how a deer can rotate its ears. Do the same with your body. Stand in place and rotate slowly with your ears cupped. When the sound seems loudest, the direction your cupped ears point is the direction of the sound's source.

You can pinpoint this direction further by cupping one ear with both hands. Think one of those old-fashioned listening cones. Point your hand-cone toward the sound. Adjust your head angle until the sound is loudest. That will give you the sound's precise angle and direction. You can then combine volume with visual clues (using binoculars if needed) to estimate distance.

TRY THIS — MAKE A SOUND MAP

To practice three-dimensional listening, draw a Sound Map.

Sound Maps challenge you not just to identify sounds, but to locate them in space.

To make a Sound Map, bring a pencil and paper outside. Find a spot away from crowds and sit.

In the center of your paper, draw a small circle and write "me" in it. That's where you're sitting. The rest of the paper represents the area around you.

I made this Sound Map in a nature preserve one November afternoon. I heard the rustling leaves and vehicles on the road almost immediately. But it took several minutes before my ears became sensitive enough to notice the small stream in the distance and the gentle breeze blowing past me. Author illustration

Sit still and make as little sound as possible. Focus not with your eyes, but with your ears. Look at your paper, not the landscape.

When you hear a sound, estimate where it came from. Then draw a picture of what made the sound relative to your "me" circle. Suppose you hear a cardinal to your left. Draw a picture of a bird on the left side of your paper.

The drawings don't have to be accurate. You're out to catalog everything you hear, so you won't have time for detailed sketches.

If the sound is nearby, draw the picture close to your circle. If the sound came from farther away, draw it toward the paper's edge.

The longer you sit, the more you'll hear. Wildlife will get used to you and become more active. You'll also become more attuned to what you're hearing, so you'll get better at noticing sounds.

Sound Maps are deceptively simple. Looking at my crude drawing, you might even think they're childish. They aren't. They're powerful skillbuilders to improve your three-dimensional listening.

Through multiple Sound Maps, you'll get faster and more accurate at pinpointing where sounds come from. That speed is essential if you want to catch a glimpse of that rare warbler you just heard.

Each time you make a Sound Map, challenge yourself to listen for the faintest sound you can hear. Then see if you can hear something fainter. Keep going until you've heard the quietest sound you can. The more you do this, the more you'll realize how many sounds you've missed out on—and how many more you can experience when you really listen.

KNOW WHEN TO GO

Three-dimensional listening will help you notice more sounds, but it can't make animals call. To hear more birds and other wildlife, you need to understand their habits. When do they sing or call, and why do they do it? Knowing that information, you can time your nature observations to let you hear the maximum number of species.

I experienced the importance of this knowledge when I started birdwatching. It was my first spring birding season, and I desperately wanted to get outside and hear all the returning warblers and other migrants sing as they established territories and attracted mates.

The day I planned to go, I had an all-morning meeting I couldn't escape. The soonest I could hit the trail was after lunch.

I didn't think it would be a problem. It was the end of March, so even at noon it was only about 50 degrees Fahrenheit. The day was clear with low humidity. I figured it would be perfect conditions for a bird walk.

Yet from the moment I reached the trailhead, I knew something was wrong. The place was silent, as quiet as in deepest winter. Where were all the birds?

I spent an hour in the woods and walked about a mile. My route took me through a variety of landscapes from ponds to meadows to streams to old-growth pines.

In that entire walk, I hardly heard

Dusk is a good time to listen for the nasal "peent" of the American woodcock. Photo: Keith Ramos, U.S. Fish and Wildlife Service

I focus a lot on birds in this chapter, but these same listening techniques can help you hear and spot other wildlife. If birds have a "dawn chorus," frogs might just have a "night chorus." Listen for them when camping near lakes and ponds. Photo: Dulcey Lima on Unsplash

a peep. The few calls I did hear were weak and half-hearted. A chickadee sang its name once. A goldfinch whined a few notes. A song sparrow got as far as its initial triplet before giving up.

Afternoons are miserable times to listen for birds. Most birds rest during the hottest part of the day— even if that heat is only 50 degrees.

I proved this point to myself by returning to that same trail the next day. This time I got there at dawn.

The woods were raucous from the start. Red-winged blackbirds, robins, and song sparrows carried on. Farther along I heard finches, chickadees, and mourning doves. I saw my first bluebirds of the season. I flushed a grouse. I even heard a screech owl.

I added up the different birds I'd seen or heard that morning and compared it with the previous afternoon. I came up with twelve species on the morning hike compared with three from the afternoon. Where I'd seen almost no birds the previous day, this time the total number was too high to count.

Birders call this phenomenon the "dawn chorus" because so many species sing that it really does sound like natural music. If you want to experience the most birdsong, get outside early. If possible, get into place before dawn. That way the birds will be used to your presence by the time they start singing.

If you don't want such an early start, stay out late instead. Many birds and other wildlife become active again at dusk. This is also a great time to hear nocturnal birds like owls and whip-poor-wills.

For the best dusk listening ex-perience, visit a local pond, marsh, or other wetland. As well as the

Owls sleep during the day, so you may not see them on your adventures. But if you go out at dusk or dawn, you stand a good chance of hearing them.

You don't have to travel to the middle of nowhere to listen for owls. Many city parks host guided "Owl Prowls." I highly recommend them, whether you're new to birding or a longtime bird lover.

Before you go owling, learn their calls. You'll be exploring after dark, so you won't be able to consult a field guide. Don't expect to learn just hoots, either. Some owls hoot, but most call with a complex mix of sounds including screeches, sighs, and snorts.

Critically important: when you go owling, don't use audio recordings to lure owls to you. Recordings confuse the birds and distract them from nesting or hunting.

In the main text, I recommend spring as the best season to hear most birds. That doesn't apply for owls. They breed in winter, so they sing the most between December and February.

If you want to see owls and not just hear them, practice the night-vision tips I described in the last chapter. Go out on a night with a full moon too. The extra light will make it easier to spot an owl once you hear its call.

Finally, keep your flashlight in your pack. Apart from ruining your night vision, a flashlight's glare can make an owl panic.

Winter months make the best owling. Apart from calling more, owls will be more active and easier to spot against the snow. Photo: Magalie St-Hilaire Poulin on Unsplash

many water birds, you may catch the "peent" sound of the male American woodcock. Track down that call, and you may witness the woodcock's elaborate flight display.

Beyond birds, wetlands are also excellent places to hear frogs. Keep your ears out for spring peepers and American bullfrogs, among other species.

SEASON MATTERS TOO

I made another mistake in that late March bird walk. Not only did I go too late in the day, but I also went too early in the season.

As a child, you probably learned that birds sing in the springtime. That's true for many species, but it's not very specific. Even within spring, different birds sing at different times.

Why? Because they return at different times. Some, like red-winged blackbirds, don't migrate at all. That's why they start calling so early. One warm winter, I remember hearing them as early as February. Other residents, like song sparrows, also start up sooner.

But to hear birds that make the long-distance flight from wintering spots in Central or South America, you'll need to wait. If these birds leave their wintering grounds too soon, they risk not finding enough food if there's a late frost.

Some of these birds can be particularly late arrivals. In my area, for example, orioles usually don't show up until May.

When should you hit the woods

Early spring—before leaf out—is ideal birding time. The bare trees make birds easier to spot. Combine three-dimensional listening and vision to find even camouflaged birds like this tiny house wren. Author photo

in search of birds? The best approach is to go multiple times throughout the spring. In March you can hear the residents. April brings the first migrants, and May brings the stragglers. By June, though, most birds have settled in to nest, so you won't hear as many songs in the summer months.

If you can't get out multiple times, I recommend April as the best getaway time. By April many spring migrants have arrived, but in most places the trees haven't leafed out yet. Use your three-dimensional listening to find the new arrivals, and then apply three-dimensional vision to spot them quickly in the bare branches.

LEARNING BIRD CALLS

Suppose I took two people and stuck them side by side in a

springtime forest at dawn. One is a typical hiker. The other is a professional ornithologist.

In theory, they should hear the same things. Sound is just pressure waves after all. The same waves will reach all four ears.

But if I asked those two people to talk about what they heard, I would get very different answers. For certain, the ornithologist will have heard more birds.

Why? It has nothing to do with their hearing. It has to do with how their brains process that information. Neuroscience backs up Goethe's quote from Chapter 1: you can hear "only what you understand."

For decades brain researchers have studied what separates experts in a field from novices. They've looked in particular at chess grandmasters. What they find is that experts literally see the world differently from us normal folks.

If I set up a chess board and had you stare at it, you might later recall the positions of a few pieces. If I showed that same chess board to a grandmaster, that person would recall nearly the entire board.

Chess grandmasters can pick out the subtle patterns and meanings behind the arrangement of pieces on a chessboard. That understanding lets them notice and remember more of it.

The same applies to birds and listening. If you don't know which birds are calling, they will tend to meld together.

Let me tell you about the day I became a birder. By sheer luck, I was walking in a nature preserve early one morning in late April. The woods rang with dozens of bird species.

At one point on my walk, I stopped. I had one of those rare epiphany moments. I realized I'd hiked more than a mile through this amazing music—and I'd been tuning it out the whole time. Because I couldn't tell the birds apart, my brain merged all the songs into a single background noise and filtered it out.

What a world I was missing!

I became determined to fix that. I never again want to walk amid such beauty and not be able to experience it.

Learning bird calls can be intimidating. Global birding checklists put the number of bird species at 10,000, and some research suggests

Nervous about learning bird calls? Start with the most common species in your area. One of the first I learned was the red-winged blackbird—a common bird with a loud, instantly memorable, "Konk-a-REEE!" Author photo

the number may be double that.

But don't let numbers scare you off. Learning birdsong isn't a test. Yes, if I put you in the woods with an ornithologist, that person would hear more birds than you would. They'd hear more birds than I would, too. You and I will probably never get to that level, but we can still improve.

I know I hear more birds now than I did that fateful April morning. It's not about reaching a goal. It's about doing better than you did last spring, or even on your last walk. Have you learned one species? That's better than knowing zero!

If you're starting out learning birdsongs, begin with the most common species in your area. It isn't silly to spend time learning calls for robins, starlings, and crows. These common species give you a chance to practice, because you'll hear them all the time. Work your way up to rarer species.

Also take advantage of the many excellent bird call learning guides out there. The guide I found most useful as a novice was the Peterson Guide's *Birding by Ear* series.

What I loved about it is that it doesn't just play the name of the bird and the song. Instead, it provides mnemonics to aid recall. It also groups similar-sounding birds together to help you learn the differences between them.

Don't limit your learning to recordings. Use your outdoor obser-vations. Ask almost any birder the best way to memorize a bird's song,

Another fun animal to listen for? Red squirrels. These fearless critters will bark and chirp at any threat that enters their territory. Their sharp, staccato burst lets you know you've entered their home. Author photo

and they'll tell you some variation of the following story.

You're outside, and you hear a song you don't recognize. Instead of saying, "Oh well, I don't know that one," you seek it out. You use three-dimensional listening to home in the bird's location, then find it in your binoculars or spotting scope.

If you can't see it, you follow the sound and get as close as you can. You do what it takes to get eyes on that bird. You may be able to identify it by sight. If not, you note features like colors, tufts, and size.

Why go to all this trouble? Two reasons. First, it's hard to identify a bird later by sound alone. A Google search for "what bird goes tweedle-dee-dum-dee-dum?" isn't likely to help you. But with visual cues, you can thumb through a field guide or

Apps and bird call recordings are important, but when it comes to memorizing bird songs, there's no substitute for getting out there and following a bird's song back to its source. Photo: Annie Spratt on Unsplash

use the Merlin app I mentioned in Chapter 3 to find the species.

Second, and more important, pursuing that bird is an experience that will stay with you. The thrill of the chase—and the success when you finally identify the bird—will cement that bird in your memory. Whenever you hear that call again, you'll remember your experience tearing through the brush to find it. That's a far more powerful memory than listening to a recording.

UNDERSTANDING AND CONNECTING WITH WILDLIFE

Many beginning birders make a critical mistake in learning songs. They focus so much on which species go with which sounds that they forget to learn what those sounds mean. They memorize a call and move on, as though they've learned everything there is to know about that bird.

Don't restrict yourself to rote memorization. Birdsongs are languages. Knowing a language you're hearing is Spanish tells you a little, but it doesn't tell you nearly as much as if you could interpret the individual words.

Birds talk to each other about all sorts of topics. Ornithologists divide these communications into two groups: songs and calls. We often use these terms interchangeably, but technically they have different meanings.

Songs relate to mating. Birds use them to attract mates. Typically males sing, although in some species both males and females sing. The northern cardinal is a good example of that.

Calls cover all the other vocalizations birds make. Some calls are territorial. They tell other birds to stay away. Others are alarms that alert neighboring birds to a predator.

Consider the chickadee. Chickadees are common sights at backyard feeders throughout North America. If you live in an area with chickadees, you've probably heard their two major vocalizations. The first says their name: "Chick-a-dee-dee-dee." The second, depending on the species, is either a two note "Phoe-be" or four-note "Phoe-boo-bee-bay."

Only one of these is the chickadee's song. Chickadees use their "Phoebe" song to attract potential mates. Male chickadees—and occasionally females—will sing this song beginning in mid-January and sing it more as winter goes on.

By contrast, the "Chick-a-dee" call functions as a signal. It lets other chickadees know where the bird is.

In other contexts, it can spread the word about a food source, warn of a nearby predator, or give an "all clear" that it's all right to come out and start eating again.

The number of "dee's" at the end gives a rough indication of how worried the bird is. The more "dee's" you hear, the greater the bird's alarm.

It's easy to focus on songs when birding. As the name suggests, they're typically more musical than calls. They're easier to distinguish between species too. But calls often tell you as much as songs, and sometimes they reveal more about a bird's behavior and environment than songs ever could.

Alarm calls are a perfect example. My neighborhood has a resident red-tailed hawk. I always know when it's near my house, not because of the hawk's call, but because of the blue jays'. When I hear a group of blue jays squawk their loud "Jay! Jay!" and go crashing through the trees, I know they're chasing the red-tail to scare it away. Those are moments I grab the binoculars.

As you learn more songs and calls, take the time to learn not just the sounds a species makes, but why it makes them. You'll deepen your appreciation for that species, which in turn will make that bird's sounds easier to remember and identify.

Knowing a bird's alarm call can help you locate other wildlife, especially predators. If you hear loud, repeated rasping or chattering from this Carolina wren, scan the area for hawks and cats. Author photo

Beyond songs and calls, also learn as much as you can about each bird's habits. Where does it like to live? What does it eat? Does it hang out near the ground, or does it spend most of its time in treetops? Knowing that information will help you hear and see more birds.

Let me give you an example. My favorite bird is the chestnut-sided warbler. I don't know why. I think it's how friendly their song sounds: "Very-very-pleased-ta-MEET-cha!" I can't possibly dislike a bird that greets me so warmly.

I love taking nature photos, and I really wanted to add a picture of a chestnut-sided warbler to my collection. So one spring, once I knew they had arrived and would be calling, I went in search of one.

I went to my local nature preserve, which is one of the few areas in the Northeast that still has old-growth forest and makes excellent bird habitat. Nothing. Other forests I commonly visit similarly had lots of birds, but no chestnut-sided warblers.

I was getting frustrated. Then I remembered something I'd read about chestnut-sided warblers. They love young forests—brushy areas of shrubs and sapling trees. They're particularly fond of old clearcut logging sites.

Chestnut-sided warblers prefer young forests because these birds nest close to the ground. The thick plants conceal their nests from predators. The insects they love to eat are also common in these places. Author photo

Knowing an animal's habitat—where it lives, what it eats—gives you a far greater chance of finding that animal. Remembering the chestnut-sided warblers' habitat allowed me to hear and photograph my favorite bird. Author photo

As it happened, a game land nearby had done some small clearcuts about five years prior. I drove out there the following weekend.

I didn't get ten feet back on the trail before I heard what I'd spent all spring listening for:

"Very-very-pleased-ta-MEET-cha!"

Chestnut-sided warblers were all over the place. I counted more than a dozen within a thousand feet of trail. And yes, I got my picture.

How do you learn an animal's habits? A good resource for birds comes from the Cornell Lab of Ornithology: AllAboutBirds.org.

This resource includes identifying information, pictures, audio recordings, range maps, and life histories for thousands of bird species. Better still, it explains in simple terms what the songs and calls for each bird mean as well as which habitat types you're most likely to see them in.

For all the information All About Birds has, don't depend on it exclusively. When it comes to acquiring knowledge of an animal's habits, there's no substitute for time outside.

The more places you practice Deep Nature Observation, the more you'll come to learn where and when you should go to see the most variety or the rarest species in your area. Use online resources to kickstart your knowledge, then hit the woods and teach the so-called "experts" something they don't know.

To practice communicating with wildlife, learn a skill from turkey hunters: call in a turkey.

Hunters typically hunt turkeys using bows or shotguns, which have short ranges. To compensate, hunters draw in male turkeys by convincing them another turkey is nearby. They use a device that mimics the sound of either a female (that the male would want to mate with) or a male (that the male would want to fight). When the turkey comes in close, the hunter shoots.

You can do this, no gun required. I use a camera.

You will need a few supplies from the world of hunting. First, you need camouflage clothes, because turkeys have excellent vision. A comfortable sitting pad helps too, since you'll spend a long time on the ground.

Your most important gear is the turkey call itself. There are several kinds, from simple push-button calls to hollow wooden boxes to diaphragms you put in your mouth.

For beginners, I recommend the box call. Push-buttons are easier to use, but they only make one sound. That won't allow for a conversation.

That conversation is what makes turkey calling such great listening practice. To call a turkey, you literally need to talk with a bird. It isn't good enough to repeat the same call. Turkey are social. If someone kept repeating the same words to you, you'd get annoyed and leave. Turkeys will do the same.

To call a turkey, get outside before dawn. Position yourself in the woods just inside a field with some scattered trees. Sit with your back against a tree and face out into the field.

As the turkeys wake and come down from their roosts in the trees, they'll start calling to each other. Join in. Keep still and quiet, except for your call.

The best season to call turkeys is spring, when they're mating. Unfortunately, spring is also when most places have their turkey hunting season, so you do need to practice hunter safety even though you don't plan to shoot anything.

To reduce the risk of hunting accidents, never wear anything red, white, or blue, because turkeys sport these colors. Don't wave or make other large movements that could be misinterpreted as a turkey. If your state has laws about wearing safety orange during hunting season, abide by them.

If all this sounds a bit boring, remember that you can do more than just call turkeys while you sit there. Since you'll be camouflaged, quiet, and motionless, use the time to engage in other aspects of Deep Nature Observation. Other animals will forget your presence and become more active.

Seize that opportunity. Listen to spring birds. Watch for other wildlife to wander by. A friend of mine tells the story of the time he went turkey hunting, and a porcupine crawled over his legs. The porcupine never realized he was there.

Chapter 6

SMELL

It is not so much for its beauty that the forest makes its claim upon men's hearts, as for that subtle something, that quality of the air, that emanation from the old trees, that so wonderfully changes and renews a weary spirit.
– Robert Louis Stevenson

Of all the senses in this book, this chapter's was the hardest to write. Smell is perhaps our most neglected sense. Suppose you had to give up one sense. Which one would you choose? Eyesight? Hearing? Not likely. What about never tasting food again or feeling anything? Those would be tough to lose. But smell…sure you'd miss out on the sweet aromas of flowers or heady scent of pine needles, but you'd get by. Your daily life probably wouldn't change much.

That's really a shame, because our sense of smell is amazing. Remember how I said we can differentiate one million colors? A 2014 study in *Nature* found that we can separate one trillion smells.[1]

For all its lack of attention, our sense of smell may be our most primal sense—the one that connects us most to our fellow mammals.

Lots of mammals are scent-oriented. A dog uses its nose to navigate its world even more than its eyes. It identifies other dogs by their unique scents, just as we identify each other by our unique faces. There is an entire universe of odors out there, yet we devote little time or energy to them.

We don't even have good words to describe scents. Usually we pick words that have a taste connection. A lemon smells sour because it tastes sour. But words that are purely about smells? Those are in short supply.

Hence the challenge for me as a writer trying to encourage you to dig deeper into your sense of smell. I don't have one trillion words for the one trillion smells you can detect.

Despite those challenges, I want to take a stab at opening up a new world of smells for you. Because our most primal sense has the power to instantly transport us in ways other senses cannot.

Although our sense of smell can't compete with a dog's, it still has a deep connection in our brains and is closely linked with taste, memory, and well-being. Photo: Georgia de Lotz on Unsplash

SMELL AND MEMORY

Whether or not we realize it, certain smells leave lasting impressions on us. That's because smell connects with memory and emotion in powerful ways.

Think of strong memories in your life. There's usually a smell attached to them. When you smell that smell, it can put you back in that moment with vivid recall.

These smells vary from person to person. The yeasty smell of home-made bread always reminds me of my grandmother and her tiny kitchen, because she loved to bake bread with me when I visited her.

The savory smell of bacon has a more negative effect on me. It was what I was cooking when I got the call that my father had passed away suddenly. That was more than a decade ago. I've hardly cooked bacon since.

Even smells most people hate can become appealing to you if they connect to a positive memory. Most people would say that cow manure is a miserable stench. But as someone who spent the first seven years of his life on a dairy farm, I find the smell oddly pleasant. It transports me back to that childhood innocence, running in the fields and playing in the barn.

What smells are like that for you? Have you ever really thought about

TRY THIS — THE SCENT LINEUP

Before going out in nature to do some smelling, take time at home to reacquaint yourself with this neglected sense. Gather a selection of objects from your house. Choose a mix of strong odors and weaker ones. Foods work perfectly, because taste and smell are so intertwined.

Line your items up on a counter. You can line them up a few different ways. One way is to have someone else arrange them without you looking. Then, wearing a blindfold, try to identify each item by smell alone.

Another option is to alternate weak and strong scents. Your nose will identify strong scents like oranges quickly, but it will need to work harder to pick out weaker smells like paper.

Once you get good at identifying smells in your house, take the scent lineup outside. Gather natural items like flowers, leaves, pine needles, and berries, then try to identify them by scent.

You may not be able to separate sugar maple leaves from red maple leaves, but this exercise will help you remember that everything in nature has a smell—one worth pausing to notice.

If you're looking for extra fun in this natural scent lineup, pick items with distinct, if not always pleasant, odors. Scrape some bark off a sweet birch stem and give the tissue underneath a whiff. You'll get a strong wintergreen scent. Crushing the leaves will also release this smell. Cherry tree twigs will often have a bitter almond scent when crushed.

Perhaps my favorite: pluck a leaflet off the invasive Tree of Heaven and give its base a whiff. It smells like rancid peanut butter. It's a great trick to play on unsuspecting fellow nature observers…not that I would ever encourage you to do such a thing, of course.

Pine needles have a recognizable scent, especially if you typically have a live Christmas tree. Photo: Susanne Alexander on Unsplash

it? Maybe not, but I'll bet you have at least a few with similar effects. They pull you back to happier times, or sadder ones.

Become aware of those smells. Write them down along with why you identify with them so strongly. Then seek them out, as you need them, when you need a pick-me-up or feel like reminiscing.

SMELL AND HEALTH

Not only can certain odors conjure memories and emotions, they can also affect our health.

If that seems impossible, bear in mind how smell works. It's different from sight or sound. With those, you interpret light or air waves. But you detect odors when molecules from the substance come in contact with sensors inside your nose. That means when I talk about breathing in the scent of pines, you're literally breathing in pine needles—or at least, tiny pieces of them.

But how can those tiny pieces affect our health? Forest bathing researchers sought to identify the source. And they found it: an airborne chemical plants release called a "phytoncide."

For those who don't speak ancient Greek, "phyton" means "plant," and "cide" means "kill." Phytoncides are chemicals that plants use to trigger their defense systems and kill their enemies.

Suppose you're a plant. You can't

Smells can trigger powerful feelings of nostalgia, for good or bad. I strangely don't mind the pungent smell of cows, since it reminds me of my childhood on a farm. Photo: Gabriel Porras on Unsplash

run. You can't scream. If an insect starts eating you, how do you let your fellow plants know there's a dangerous pest about? You do it with chemicals.

When under attack, plants release phytoncides. Other plants receive the phytoncide signal and use it as a call to prepare their own internal defenses.

Insect plant eaters are some of the most common animals in the world. So plants, especially trees, release a lot of phytoncides.

Conifers—think pines, spruces, firs, and the like—release more phytoncides than broad-leaved trees. That's why the odor of a deep, old pine forest is so strong.

But here's where that odor becomes interesting. It turns out that just as a tree's phytoncides trigger immune responses in fellow plants, our bodies respond to them as well.

Our immune system reacts to these chemicals by increasing production of natural killer cells— the cells that fight diseases. It also increases the presence of certain anti-cancer proteins.

Remember that immune-boosting forest bathing research I talked about in Chapter 2? It was participants' sense of smell, absorbing all those phytoncide triggers, that stimulated their immune systems.

You can get these same benefits simply by walking in a forest, especially a conifer forest. Walk slowly and take long, deep breaths through your nose. That will maximize the intake of phytoncides.

Want a nature health supercharge? Walk through an old conifer forest after it rains. The rain releases phytoncides from the trees. Breathing in these phytoncides boosts our immune response. Photo: Brandon Molitwenik on Unsplash

One of the best times to take up phytoncides is just after a summer rain. The rain volatilizes plant oils that have settled on the ground. These oils contain phytoncides. As a result, those phytoncides get swept into the air at a much higher concentration than normal.

This high concentration of phytoncides gives the just-rained-on forest a unique earthy smell. It's called "petrichor" For the non-Greeks again, "petri" means "stone," and "ichor" means "essence."

It isn't only the presence of phytoncides that make the forest scent good for our health. Trees are also powerful air filters. Just by living, they take in carbon dioxide and release oxygen, which we need to breathe. The concentration of oxygen in a forest can be detectably higher than in a city. While in a forest, you can literally breathe easier.

Trees also draw many pollutants from the air that otherwise make us sick. In 2014, researchers from the U.S. Forest Service found that in the lower 48 U.S. states alone, trees and forests remove more than 17 million tons of air pollution every year. They calculated that this reduction in air pollution prevents 670,000 cases of acute respiratory symptoms annually.[2]

When we lose trees, the health impacts are potent—and even lethal. In the U.S., millions of ash trees have died because of an invasive insect called the emerald ash borer. Prior to the borer, ash were common

street trees in many U.S. cities.

In a grim study, the U.S. Forest Service looked at counties across 15 states where large numbers of ash trees had died. They compared mortality rates before and after the emerald ash borer swept through the counties. The loss of ash trees in these counties was associated with more than 21,000 deaths related to respiratory and cardiovascular disease.[3]

AROMATHERAPY

If you can't get out to a deep pine forest to take in phytoncides, you can gain some of the benefits at home by diffusing certain essential oils. As with natural forests, conifers like Scots pine, Douglas fir, and especially cedar make good choices for oil diffusion.

You can make your own aromatherapy diffuser with a few ingredients. First you'll need a small jar to

Trees are natural air filters, so when a lot of them die, it has noticeable effects on human health. The loss of ash trees to the invasive emerald ash borer has contributed to tens of thousands of deaths. Photos: Author photo (left), U.S. Department of Agriculture (right)

TRY THIS — GET SOME HOUSEPLANTS

Another way to get some of the health benefits of nature's smell is to bring nature into your home or workspace using houseplants.

Despite our many filters, indoor air quality is usually worse than outdoor air quality. Often, not enough air exchange happens with the outside. As a result, indoor air pollutants like volatile organic compounds from paint and carpeting build up inside with no way to escape.

Depending on where you live, the indoor air quality in your home or office can be as much as five times worse than the air you breathe outside.

Houseplants reduce concentrations of these pollutants. They take up many indoor toxic chemicals as part of photosynthesis.

No less a body than NASA has studied this phenomenon. In 1989, they were investigating ways to refresh the air quality in space stations. They identified houseplants that work best for improving indoor air quality.[4]

In general, seek bigger, leafier plants. A few options include peace lily, English ivy, snake plant, azalea, red-edge dracaena, bamboo palm, and golden pothos.

Pothos and snake plants in particular make great choices. Apart from their air-purifying power, they're easy to care for. Just be careful if you have pets, as some houseplants can be toxic to them if ingested.

Houseplants also have documented mental health benefits. They reduce stress for those around them and increase energy levels.[5]

You don't need to turn your home or office into a jungle to get these impacts. While there is no recommended amount per se, the lead author on the NASA study told *Time* magazine that he suggests two good-sized plants per 100 square feet of interior space.[6]

A few houseplants can have significant benefits for your home or office's indoor air quality. They also liven up a space and improve your mood. Photo: Annie Spratt on Unsplash

hold the oil. Glass or ceramic can work. It doesn't need to be anything fancy.

You can buy diffuser jars at many home supply stores, but look for cheaper options around the house or at thrift stores first. The only real requirements are that the jar be watertight and have a narrow top to keep your oils from evaporating too quickly.

Next you'll need something the liquid can travel up and diffuse through. Bamboo skewers work well for this. They're long yet thin, so they'll fit easily into that narrow opening in your jar. Cut the skewers

Natural essential oils, especially from conifers, can give you some of the health benefits of a forest walk. Photo: Mary Skrynnikova on Unsplash

so they are about twice the height of your diffusing jar.

With your jar set up, you'll need the oil next. You can use just one or make a mixture. Experiment with different kinds and find a scent you consider pleasing. Cedar oil is a great place to start.

Don't put the straight essential oil in the jar. Instead, mix it with another oil (called a carrier oil) or vodka diluted with some water. You can use mineral oil as your base, but if you'd rather avoid petroleum-based oils, sweet almond or safflower oil also work.

If you use alcohol, be aware that it will evaporate more quickly than oil. Expect to go through more essential oil using it.

If using oil as your base, start with a mix of 30 percent essential oil to 70 percent base oil. For vodka, add about 25 drops of essential oil to a ¼ cup of your vodka and water mix.

It's better if your initial concentration is too weak. You can always add a few more drops of essential oil later if you need a bigger scent kick.

Pour your oil mix in your jar, then add the bamboo skewers. Let it sit for a couple hours to give the oils time to saturate into the skewers. Come back and rotate the skewers so the saturated ends poke out of the jar.

Now you're all set. The essential oils will wick up through the skewers and diffuse into the air. Rotate which end of the skewers sit in the oil about once each week.

Done correctly, the scent from

The majesty, roar, and fresh smell of a waterfall are all I need to boost my mood. Author photo

your diffuser should be noticeable but not strong. If it's overpowering, add a little more base oil to dilute the essential oil. You can also try a jar with a narrower opening.

Diffusers are good ways to get exposure to essential oils without needing electricity or candles. That makes them excellent choices for both office spaces and homes with children. That said, you don't want your kids or animals drinking the liquid in the diffuser, so keep your diffuser out of reach of any pets or children.

THE SMELL OF WATER

Plants aren't the only smell that can invigorate you in nature. Water also has that power. It doesn't use phytoncides. It uses negative ions in the air.

Ions happen all the time in nature. They result when a molecule has either more protons than electrons (creating a positive charge) or when it has more electrons than protons (creating a negative charge).

More than 80 years of research has investigated whether these charges play a role in human health. If you go online, you'll find influencers extolling the benefits of negative ions in particular. Positive ions are supposedly associated with heightened anxiety and irritability, while negative ions are healthy and reduce stress.

Unfortunately, a lot of the "science" on negative ions is junk, and even the good studies are inconclusive. In 2013, a study published in the journal *BioMed Central Psychiatry* pooled results from thirty-three air ionization health studies spanning from 1957 to 2012. They found no effects for anxiety, mood, sleep, or personal comfort from exposure either to positive or negative ions.[7]

That said, the researchers did find one health benefit from negative ions. Across all the studies, they found exposure to negative ions significantly lowered depression ratings, and higher concentrations of negative ions enhanced the benefit.

Exposure even to low levels of negative ions significantly improved depression symptoms in those suffering seasonal depression, like seasonal affective disorder. High levels improved symptoms for both seasonal and chronic depression sufferers.

What does all this have to do with water? Water, particularly moving water, generates a lot of negative ions. The faster the water, the more negative ions generated.

Thanks to this trait, the air around a waterfall can have up to a thousand times the concentration of negative ions as the air in a typical home or office. When you visit a waterfall and breathe in that air, you're taking in those ions and gaining a natural ally against depression.

Suppose you don't have a waterfall near you. No problem. Any moving water will disperse negative ions into the air. Find a forested stream and walk along its banks. Pick one that moves quickly, with a lot of obstacles in the water like rocks and fallen logs. The rushing, churning water will release more ions. At the same time, you'll also be exposed to the healing air of the trees along the stream.

Don't forget too that as much as these places promote good health, they're also excellent spots to engage in Deep Nature Observation. Forested streams concentrate life. They provide food, water, and shelter close together, so many wildlife spend much of their lives near these places.

While you're breathing deep and savoring the healthful smells of the trees and water, also listen for birds. Keep your eyes open for wildflowers. Turn over some stream rocks and handle some insects.

Curious how to do that? We'll talk about that next.

Speaking of natural smells and health benefits, we can't forget to mention the ocean. One breath of that salty sea air instantly lifts my spirits. Photo: Joel Vodell on Unsplash

Chapter 7

TOUCH

One touch of nature makes the whole world kin.
– William Shakespeare

Most of our senses have a narrow window to the outside. We see with our eyes. We smell with our nose. We hear with our ears. We taste with our tongue. But one sense—touch—is different. With touch, your whole body becomes a sense organ.

Most of the time, though, we don't think of it that way. We focus on what we feel with our hands. We also tend to focus on solid objects—items we can rub our hands on or pick up.

But there's so much more out there we can feel. How about weather? The sun's warmth on your face, cool rain dripping on your arms, temperature, humidity, air pressure…we sense all these phenomena through touch.

Back in Chapter 3, when I talked about gear, I left footwear out of my discussion. That was on purpose. Common advice for outdoor adventuring is to wear sturdy shoes or boots. When I go for walks in the woods, I prefer waterproof hiking shoes, largely because nothing ruins a walk faster for me than soaked socks.

But with Deep Nature Observation, you aren't really walking. You aren't headed for a destination, and you aren't moving quickly. That means we can relax the rules on outdoor footwear a bit. Flip-flops and sandals are acceptable Deep Nature Observation footwear. That way, any time you feel like it, you can remove them and feel the earth directly through your feet.

When's the last time your feet actually touched the ground? Think about that for a moment. It may well have been years. Even if you walk barefoot inside, you have a floor between you and the planet. When we go outside, we put on shoes.

If we're barefoot outside, we're usually at a place like a pool that has a concrete floor. Other than the beach, there aren't many places where we let our feet and the earth connect.

That's a loss for us, and I don't mean in the spiritual, "we have lost our connection with Mother Earth" way. I'm talking a physical loss.

There is growing evidence of a literal electric connection that occurs between the ground and people. The Earth's surface has a negative charge. Because we spent nearly all our history walking barefoot, our bodies are adapted to be in contact with that charge. When we wear rubber shoes, we block that connection.

Research is still spotty, because the concept of a health connection from walking barefoot is still a new idea. But evidence from multiple studies suggests barefoot walking may improve sleep. Contact with the earth may help you fall asleep faster, sleep more deeply, and wake feeling more rested and less stiff than you would otherwise.[1]

This research has led to a trend known as "earthing" or "grounding" among some outdoor recreationists. Children know it as "kicking off your shoes and romping in the grass." Give it a try.

If you aren't comfortable walking barefoot outside, ease into it. Leather sandals won't block Earth's electrical connection, so you can wear those instead of going barefoot while getting similar results.

Of course, from a Deep Nature Observation perspective, wearing sandals limits how much of the Earth you'll feel through your feet. For that reason, I still prefer ditching footwear altogether as long as you feel safe doing so.

You don't need to spend your whole Deep Nature Observation experience barefoot. A few minutes on a patch of bare soil, leaf litter, or lawn is enough.

I do have one safety caution with barefoot walking, and it has nothing to do with sharp objects. Your slow, methodical, Deep Nature Observation pace should help avoid those. When you're done barefoot walking, check your feet for ticks. Earthing may help you sleep, but it's not worth getting Lyme Disease over.

Walking barefoot outside can make a powerful connection with nature. Photo: David L. Smith on Unsplash

TRY THIS — GET DRENCHED IN THE RAIN

In our daily lives, even a light rain sends us scurrying for the nearest doorway or overhang. But when it comes to Deep Nature Observation, few outside activities will better remind you that your whole body is a sense organ than to let yourself get soaked in the rain.

A spontaneous drenching can be fun, but this is a case where some preparation can help a lot. Pack a towel and second set of clothes in a waterproof bag. That way you can dry off and change when you're done.

You don't have to just stand in the rain either. Go for a walk. Or—if you can get past the weirdness of it—lie on the ground and let the full might of the rain wash over you.

This activity may sound extreme, but it's a powerful feeling to let nature literally wash over you. Photo: Gage Walker on Unsplash

Lying in the rain takes the idea of barefoot walking to its extreme. Walking barefoot reconnects our bodies with nature. It permits us to touch nature in a way we rarely let ourselves do. Both it and lying in the rain seem like they should be completely wrong. And yet, for connecting with the world, they can be perfectly right.

But what's the point of lying in the rain? It gets at several of the mindsets I encourage you to adopt in Deep Nature Observation. First, it overcomes sensory numbness. Your entire body will feel the rain. It will feel unpleasant to start. Work through those initial sensations, though, and you'll find yourself feeling oddly free. You're doing something so out of the box, so unlike what society says you should do, that it will liberate you in a way not many experiences can.

Lying in the rain is also a good way to practice soft fascination. You'll have all these thoughts at first about how crazy this experience is. Again, work through those. Try not to judge the experience. Instead, just let yourself experience the moment, without thought or analysis.

Finally, lying in the rain is an intimate way to connect with nature. As we'll talk about in a couple chapters, it's a way to induce feelings of oneness with the world that can be immensely gratifying.

NATIVE PLANT GARDENING

You don't need to barefoot walk to make a physical connection with the earth. One of the best tactile connections you can get with nature is to work with soil.

If you're a gardener, you already know this. Gardening forms about as intimate a relationship with nature as you can get. Instead of just observing your environment, you're actively participating in it. You're literally getting your hands dirty to nurture plants and help them grow.

That close connection has benefits for you too. A common soil bacteria, *Mycobacterium vaccae*, has the power to make you both healthier and happier.

How is that possible? Like many scientific discoveries, we learned it by accident.

Researchers were testing to see whether this soil bacterium helped

Gardening with native plants helps support invertebrates, which in turn provide an important protein source for many birds like this black-capped chickadee. Author photo

fight lung cancer. It didn't, but there was a positive side effect. The patients reported an improved quality of life.

The researchers explored that finding by injecting the soil bacterium into sick mice. They found the mice behaved as though they were on antidepressants.[2]

The researchers concluded that a strong link exists between our immune systems and our emotions. When we have healthier immune systems, we feel happier.

Mycobacterium vaccae stimulates the immune system. In the process, it boosts happiness too.

If you want to get some of this soil health boost for yourself, consider starting a native plant garden. Any garden can give you soil contact, but a native plant garden in particular will connect you with both soil and the natural world.

You see, in many ways modern gardening isn't natural at all. Most garden plants we're familiar with aren't native to where we live. Instead, they're introduced, human-developed varieties of plants from all around the globe.

Why is that a problem? First, those non-native plants offer little for wildlife. Most native plant-eating insects specialize in certain plants. If those plants aren't around, they physically can't eat anything else.

Second, non-native plants have a bad habit. They don't stay where you plant them. Instead, their seeds spread to other, often wilder areas.

Once they arrive, these plants can

Native plant gardens can be both beautiful and support wildlife, like this monarch butterfly garden at the National Conservation Training Center in West Virginia. Photo: Brett Billings, U.S. Fish and Wildlife Service

take over and become "invasive." Invasive plants overrun native ones due to their rapid growth, prolific seeds, and lack of plant eaters that can eat them and keep them in check.

Many of the worst invasive plants started as garden plants. Japanese barberry, bush honeysuckle, and multiflora rose are just three examples. Many more exist.

If you want to build a natural connection through your gardening without risking the spread of invasive plants, the best way to do it is to transition from non-native ornamentals to native plants.

But how do you do that? How do you even get started? What should you plant?

I can't give you specific advice on your native plant garden in this one section. Wherever you live, odds are there are hundreds of native plant species and many more non-native ornamentals on top of that. The native plants that are right for you depend on your climate, the kind of soil you have, and how much light your garden gets.

What I can give you, though, are some resources to get you started. PlantNative.org has native plant and nursery lists by state to help narrow down your choices. Also worth checking out are the plant lists on Wildflower.org, a website run by the Lady Bird Johnson Wildflower Center.

Finally, the Audubon Society

When planning your garden, it's useful to know your backyard's soil type. Soil is a mix of water, air, and solids, and those solids vary from place to place.

Soil solids fall into three categories based on how big the particles are: sand, silt, and clay. Sand is the biggest, silt is medium, and clay is the smallest.

The ratio of these three particles determines the kind of soil you have, known as the soil's "type."

Soil type influences what you can grow and how well it will do. Soils high in clay, for instance, hold water longer, while sandy soils drain faster. Plants that need a lot of water may struggle in sandy soils, while those that can handle drier conditions may fare better.

The ideal soil for gardeners is a mix of all three particles called "loam." It contains about 40 percent sand, 40 percent silt, and 20 percent clay.

You can figure out your soil type with nothing more than your hands and a little water. For a general assessment, use the squeeze test. Put a small handful of damp (not soaking!) soil in your hand. Now rub the soil between your fingers. Do you feel grit? That means your soil has a lot of sand. If instead the soil feels slimy, that indicates a lot of clay.

Another test you can use is the ribbon method. Again, take a handful of damp soil. Roll it between your hands until it forms a ribbon. Next, hold the ribbon by one end and lift it so it stands vertically. If it stays in one piece, you have mostly clay soil. If the ribbon breaks, you have a loam with a good mix of soil particle sizes. If you can't make a ribbon at all, your soil is at least 50 percent sand.

Determining your soil type is a good first step when gardening. Learning what your soil has—and what it needs—can give you an idea of what plants to choose and which soil amendments or fertilizers you may need. Photo: National Park Service

A native desert garden will look different from one in a wetter climate. When choosing plants for your garden, get local advice from native plant lists, cooperative extension offices, and local nurseries.
Photo: Marie Martin on Unsplash

put together an amazing resource: Audubon.org/native-plants. Type in your zip code, and the site gives you native plant ideas and local resources for wildlife-friendly gardens.

Whichever plants you choose, confirm with your nursery that they cultivated the plants, rather than collecting them from the wild. There have been instances of nurseries harvesting wild plants and raising them for sale. These plants are often marketed as "nursery grown," which is technically true but harms natural areas by removing plants from them.

TOUCHING WILDLIFE

Touching plants and working with soil are easy ways to get a tactile connection with nature. Animals are something different.

In most cases, you won't get the chance to touch wildlife. Most wild animals have a well-deserved fear of humans and will flee at your approach.

Even if they don't, in almost all cases you shouldn't touch them. An animal that seems tame can quickly become dangerous. It may have rabies, or it may have been fed in the past. It will act tame until it realizes you don't have food. At that point it can become aggressive and may bite or attack you.

That said, you can touch some wildlife safely and without harming them. Most of them are insects and other invertebrates.

Caddisfly larvae like these are relatively easy to find in small streams. They're safe to handle, so check them out and then return them to the place you found them. Photo: Ryan Hagerty, U.S. Fish and Wildlife Service

One easy place to find touchable wildlife is a fallen log. Roll it over, and you'll often find salamanders and invertebrates like millipedes living in its moist, shaded environment. Both types of critters are safe to pick up. You may also find lizard or snake eggs. Return anything you handle—including the log—to its original spot when you're done.

Another great location for friendly wildlife is in a stream. Streams—especially forested streams with cleaner water, are home to invertebrates like insect larvae, snails, clams, and crayfish. With a few simple tools, you can catch, view, and yes, handle these stream critters.

To find stream invertebrates, put on some shoes and clothes you don't mind getting wet and muddy. You'll also need a 5-gallon bucket, a disposable cake pan, and a D-frame net. This kind of net has a flat edge so you can set it flush with the stream bottom. Outdoor suppliers and large online retailers stock these nets.

Head to the cleanest stream you have access to. It helps if the stream is small and surrounded by forest. Go for something a few feet wide and a few inches deep at most.

Walk along the bank. As you walk, look for large rocks in the water, especially those that are both submerged and exposed to the air. Pick up these rocks and turn them over. You may find stonefly nymphs clinging to them.

Next, wade into the stream. Put a few inches of stream water in your bucket, then set your D-frame net just downstream of your body. Kick the streambed in front of the net. This kicking will dislodge invertebrates hiding in the streambed, and they'll get caught in your net.

Pull up your net, get out of the stream, and empty your net into your bucket. Go downstream a couple more times and repeat this process to capture more invertebrates.

When you're satisfied with your catch, find a dry spot and sit down. Transfer the critters you've found from the bucket to your cake pan by gently dumping the water into the pan.

The advantage to the cake pan is that it lets you observe the invertebrates up close. If you have a hand lens, now's an excellent time to use it. Most stream invertebrates are harmless, so feel free to pick them up and touch them. When you're done, return the critters to the stream.

HAND-FEED A BIRD

Hand-feeding wildlife is almost always a bad idea. For mammals like deer, bear, and squirrels, it teaches them that humans mean food. That can lead to wildlife attacks on people who don't have food for the animal. Those situations frequently end with someone injured and the animal dead.

Even when they don't, most human foods like corn are indigestible to wild mammals. Corn, for example, can harm and even kill white-tailed deer. The acid produced in the deer's stomach as it tries to digest the corn can eat away the stomach lining, create a tear, and kill the deer.

That said, there is one kind of animal you can hand-feed: songbirds.

Songbirds range widely for food, so they don't become habituated to human feeding the way mammals do. With some black oil sunflower seeds and a lot of patience, you can touch a wild bird.

Birds won't come to your hand right away. They'll be scared of you and fly away. To get birds to eat from your hand, you first have to get them used to your presence.

To do that, start by attracting them to your yard. Set up a birdfeeder and

Small plastic observation pails like this one are cheap and work well for close-up observation of stream critters. Some even have built-in magnifiers. Author photo

keep it stocked and cleaned. Help the birds feel safe by ridding your yard of outdoor pets. Make sure the birds have cover like a nearby bush or pine tree so they can hide if they get scared.

Now wait a few weeks. Let the birds get used to your yard.

When you have good activity at your feeder, start going outside at the same time each day. Top off your feeder, then sit or stand as still as possible ten feet away from it. Talk softly so the birds get used to your voice as well as your presence.

Eventually the birds won't be scared by you coming outside. You'll know when this happens. Instead of flying away and hiding in the trees when you come outside, birds will keep coming to the feeders.

Once the birds feel comfortable with you, stand a foot closer to the feeder each day. Instead of being ten feet away, now you're nine. The next day you're eight, and so on.

When you can stand right next to the feeder and birds still fly to it, you'll know you're ready for hand feeding.

But don't get too excited just yet. Get birds used to your hand by holding it out, palm up, on or next to the feeder. Do this for a few days to give the birds time to adjust. Once they feel comfortable eating next to your hand, empty your feeder. Place some black oil sunflower seeds in your hand and wait.

At this point it's essential that you remain absolutely still and quiet. Try not to swallow, which birds interpret as a predatory motion.

If you've followed all these steps, you may get lucky and have a few courageous birds land on your hand

For the best chance at hand-feeding a bird, start first by getting birds comfortable in your yard. Set up a feeder and keep any cats indoors. Author photo

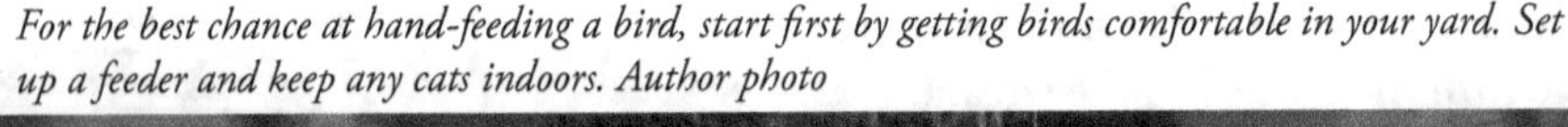

Convincing a bird to land on your hand takes a lot of luck and patience, but the payoff is an amazing experience you'll remember for a long time. Photo: Razvan Narcis Ticu on Unsplash

and eat.

Take care not to jump or startle. That's trickier to do than it sounds. You'll have that thrill of excitement that all your weeks of work have paid off. In addition, birds have pointed toes, so you may feel little pinpricks when they land and walk around on your palm. Force yourself to stay still. You can jump for joy when you get back inside the house.

A variety of birds will eat from your hand. Chickadees are your best bet, because they're curious and braver than other birds. Other common birds that will eat from your hand are nuthatches, titmice, and downy woodpeckers. All these birds are widespread and regular feeder birds in North America.

Hand-feeding birds works best in winter. Birds need a lot of calories this time of year, and their normal food supplies are less available. That combination means they'll take more risks, including sitting on your hand. Mornings also seem to work best, because birds are hungry after surviving the long, cold winter night.

Chapter 8

TASTE

To plant a garden is to believe in tomorrow.
– Audrey Hepburn

This chapter admittedly makes me nervous. In recent years, foraging wild foods has become something of a craze in the outdoor community. Videos, articles, and books play up the joys of harvesting cattail roots, mushrooms, and all manner of leaves for tea.

Despite foraging's popularity, the concept bothers me for two reasons. First, it puts yet another strain on an already overtaxed natural system. Even if it weren't for threats like climate change and invasive species, plants fight for every inch of growth. Add humans picking them, and it becomes even harder for them to survive and reproduce.

If you need proof, look at American ginseng, which has seen a big drop in its numbers because of human overharvesting. The plant is now threatened or endangered in some locations.

My second reason for disliking foraging is more practical. Yes, some wild plants are edible, but many others are poisonous. With mushrooms in particular, there's a grim saying: "If you're wrong, you're dead."

It's easy to say, "Don't eat something if you aren't certain of what it is." But the reality is that knowing basic plant identification often isn't enough. Many edible plants have poisonous look-alikes. Unless you're paying close attention, you can miss the subtle differences and accidentally eat the wrong thing.

Even if you eat the right thing, you can still wind up sick. You may have an allergy to that plant or fungus that you didn't know about. If an allergic reaction happens when you're way out in the woods, help may not reach you in time.

All this may sound like an inauspicious start to a chapter on eating wild foods. I don't intend to scare you. Foraging can be a rewarding way to experience and appreciate nature. There are ways to avoid many of the common dangers associated with foraging, and there are strategies that can reduce the risk of overharvesting wild populations.

That said, I do want you to take foraging seriously. If you engage in it, please do it with care and respect for both yourself and the natural world.

TRY THIS — FORAGE FOR BLACKBERRIES

Wild blackberries are a good beginner foraging plant. They're simple to identify, have no dangerous look-alikes, and can be eaten raw. They also have a wide range in North America.

The key to blackberry foraging is timing. Blackberries ripen in a narrow window in late summer. Depending on where you are, late August or September tend to be the best months to search for them.

Wild blackberries look a lot like farm-grown ones, only smaller. They have many small spheres that cluster into one fruit. Unripe blackberries are red and taste sour, while ripe ones turn dark purple or black and have a sweet flavor.

Raspberries also grow wild in many places, often in tandem with blackberries. You can pick and eat them raw too. Unripe raspberries will look pale green, white, or pink, while ripe raspberries look red.

You can tell ripe raspberries from unripe blackberries by picking one. A raspberry has a hollow center and looks like a little bowl. A blackberry is solid in the middle and comes off more like a cylinder.

In theory, blackberry picking is as easy as seeing some berries, plucking them off the plant, and popping them in your mouth. In practice, it's a little more difficult than that—and I have the torn jeans to prove it. With that in mind, here are some tips for safe and enjoyable blackberry picking:

Blackberries are more than tasty. They're rich in antioxidants, fiber, and vitamin C. Photo: Elizabeth George on Unsplash

The plants growing all around the man in this picture are blackberry canes. Note that they're taller than he is. When blackberry-picking, protect yourself with long sleeves and pants. You should also make noise to avoid startling bears foraging in the same patch. Author photo

- As with any wild foraging, always be certain of what you're eating. If you have any doubt about your plant identification, leave it alone.
- Also as with any wild foraging, the first time you try wild blackberries, only eat a few. See how you feel the next day. Doing this will minimize the chances of an allergic reaction or upset stomach.
- Always get landowner permission before foraging.
- Blackberries are "bramble fruits," and they deserve the name. Sharp thorns protect the berries (technically they aren't thorns, but the point is, ouch!). Guard yourself with long sleeves and durable pants.
- If you aren't sure where to look for blackberries, check open areas that get decent sun. Recent logging sites and blowdowns are great spots. Roadsides are common areas to find blackberries too, but I avoid them because of the risk of road pollutants like salt being on the berries.
- Make noise while you collect blackberries. Whistle, talk to yourself, sing a song…whatever it takes. Blackberry canes can grow over eight feet tall, so you can easily find yourself with a limited field of view. The problem with that? Bears love blackberries too. If you make noise, nearby bears will hear you, get scared, and usually leave.
- If you're collecting a lot of blackberries, bring several small containers rather than one large one. That reduces the chance that the berries will squash under their own weight.
- Leave some blackberries on the plant. You want berries in future years, and many birds and other animals rely on blackberries for food. Take no more than a quarter of the ripe berries. Leave any berries above head height for the birds.
- Foraged blackberries spoil quickly, so eat or freeze them within 24 hours of picking.

Mushrooms are a popular foraging item, but I can't recommend them. While many varieties are safe to eat, there are many poisonous ones too. The types are often difficult to tell apart, so they're a poor choice for novice foragers. Photo: Annie Spratt on Unsplash

WILD FORAGING BEST PRACTICES

The specific plants you'll forage will differ depending on where you live and the type of landscape you're visiting. I'll touch on a couple widespread examples in this chapter, but for more detail, check out one of the many excellent books on foraging. Better still, connect with local experts at nature organizations like your county's Cooperative Extension office. They may have staff who can help you identify locally edible plants.

Leaning on that experience is crucial when starting out in foraging. Go on multiple edible plant walks with several foragers. Pay close attention to any instructions about which parts of a plant are edible and under what circumstances.

Practice your plant identification extensively. Make sure you know any look-alikes for your chosen wild food. If you have any doubt, don't eat it.

Also ensure you know which parts of the plant are edible and under what circumstances. Sometimes new leaves are edible, but old ones aren't. Some plants can be eaten raw, while others must be cooked first.

Before you pick anything, make sure you have permission. In many parks, removing plants is illegal. If there are local regulations about wild harvesting in general or for certain rare plants like ginseng, follow them.

When you do take that first bite, eat only a small amount. That way if you made a mistake—or if you have an unanticipated allergy—the effects will hopefully be minor.

It helps too if you go with someone who can doublecheck your identification. And if one of you does get sick, the other can call for help or get you to a doctor more quickly than you could if you were alone.

Progress through foraging slowly. Eat only one new thing at a time. Master your identification of, say, blackberries, before you move on to leeks. Master leeks before you try brewing tea, and so forth.

Take care of the plants you harvest too. Never pick all of a plant. Otherwise it won't be able to reproduce. In populated areas where more people may forage, take less to reduce the risk of overharvesting. If a plant is rare, don't harvest it.

Above all, take the time to learn the plant's life cycle and role in the environment before you harvest it. That way, when you do harvest, you'll have respect for that plant and ensure that both the amount you take and the way you take it will not do lasting damage to the plant or its environment.

TEA FROM CONIFER NEEDLES

Many plants can be brewed into herbal teas. As with any foraging, the usable species vary from location to location. But in many places, certain conifer needles can make excellent tea. Some of these teas can be very healthy, with high levels of vitamins A and C.

As with any wild food, find out which local species are usable for tea and which aren't. Many pines and pine look-alikes are poisonous. Check with local experts for recommendations and species identification tips.

Most importantly, if you are pregnant or think you may become pregnant, do *not* drink any wild teas. Even some otherwise safe wild teas can have unpredictable

American ginseng is a cautionary tale of overharvesting wild plants. This rare plant is now protected and generally requires a permit to collect. Photo: Dan Pittillo, U.S. Fish and Wildlife Service

and occasionally dangerous side effects on pregnancies, including miscarriage.

That advice doesn't only apply to wild teas. When my wife was pregnant, our doctor advised us that she should stay away from all herbal teas, even commercially sold ones, due to the same risks.

In my part of the world, a good tea choice is eastern white pine. This long-needled pine is easy to identify because it's the only pine in my region that grows its needles in bundles of five. It's also widespread in the eastern United States and Canada.

Native Americans used eastern white pine tea to prevent scurvy. It also has purported antioxidant and immune function benefits.

Whichever species you use, you want new needles—the younger the better. Many pine trees grow all their new needles for the year in spring, so spring is the best time to brew pine needle tea.

You'll need about half a cup of young needles to make tea. White pine needles are long (as are many other pine needles), so chop them into half-inch lengths.

Needles chopped, bring three cups of water almost to a boil in a saucepan or pot. Reduce the heat to a simmer. Don't let the water boil, because boiling can release bitter compounds from the needles.

Add the needles, then cover the pot. Let the needles steep for 10-20 minutes. How long depends on taste. Start with ten minutes for your first tea. If the tea isn't strong enough, let them go longer in your next preparation.

Don't let the needles steep longer

Eastern white pine needles have a long history of use to make tea. This tree is easy to identify thanks to its long needles in bundles of five. Photo: Tadeusz Zachwiej on Unsplash

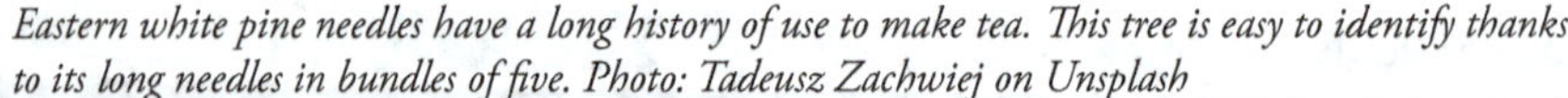

than 20 minutes. The tea can get too strong, and the vitamins can degrade.

Strain out the pine needles, then pour the tea into a mug. You can drink it hot or cold. Add a little sweetener as needed.

For an authentic wild foraged taste, use a little maple syrup as your sweetener. We'll talk about how you can get some of that in a little bit.

PICK WILD LEEKS

Wild leeks, also known as ramps or ramsons, are another good beginner foraging plant. They're easy to identify, widespread in eastern North America, and of course, tasty.

Leeks are a type of wild onion. They have a small white bulb that grows in the ground, a scallion-like stalk, and long, broad, bright green leaves. They have a flavor reminiscent of onion and garlic.

Both the leaves and bulbs of leeks are edible. The bulbs can be fried and served alongside potatoes, bacon, and eggs (a common way of serving them in Appalachia). They can also be pickled or used in soups.

Ramps have a stronger flavor than grocery store onions, so you won't need as much as you would if you were using an onion. As for the leaves, they spoil quickly and can be tough and fibrous, but you can eat them fresh by chopping them up and sautéing them or making them into a pesto.

When picking leeks, one of your advantages is that they sprout in early spring. That means fewer other

Ramps are a kind of wild onion. Both the bulb and leaves are edible. Photo: Christopher Previte on Unsplash

plants are growing, so it's easier to spot them and confirm your identification.

Look for leeks in mountainous areas, as they're more common at higher elevations. Each plant has one or two leaves measuring one to two inches wide and four to twelve inches long. Leeks often grow in patches, which makes them easier to locate while hiking.

Unfortunately, the popularity of leeks has exploded the past few years, and that popularity has led to a drop in their numbers. They're still widespread, but they're getting harder to find.

If you're going to pick leeks, be respectful of this declining plant and harvest it sustainably. Key to doing that is to leave the roots in the soil. Don't pull leeks from the ground the way you would a carrot or onion. If you just yank out the whole plant, you'll kill it.

Instead, first use a small trowel to dig around the leek just enough to expose the bulb. Next, take a sharp knife and cut horizontally through the bulb so you leave the bottom third and all the roots in the soil.

Remove the leaves and top two-thirds of the bulb and put them in a plastic bag to take home with you. Finally, cover the cut bulb and roots with soil. By doing this, the bulb can regrow next year.

Prior to leeks' popularity wave, the common advice was to take no more than one third of the leeks growing in any one patch. I don't use that advice anymore. To protect leeks for the future, take no more than one in ten of what's growing in any given patch.

GROW YOUR OWN SHIITAKE MUSHROOMS

Foraging in general has become popular with many outdoor enthusiasts, but mushrooming in particular has become something of a fascination. Ardent explorers seek out edible varieties like morels, lion's mane, and laetiporus, commonly called "chicken of the woods" for its supposed similar flavor to poultry.

As enthusiastic as many of you no doubt are about mushrooming, as an author, I'm going to let caution be the better part of valor here. I'm not going to try to teach you in one

Wild leeks, also called ramps, grow in mountainous areas from eastern Canada south to Georgia in early spring. Spot them by looking for clusters of plants, each with one or two long, broad leaves. Photo: Ryan Hagerty, U.S. Fish and Wildlife Service

small section of one chapter how to identify edible mushrooms from poisonous ones.

If you want to try mushroom foraging, I recommend you pick up some books devoted specifically to that subject. You should also find local experts who can teach you about the mushrooms you can eat in your area and the ones you should avoid.

Rather than focus on wild mushrooms, let's talk about a way you can grow your own mushrooms in a natural way. With a firewood log and some basic equipment, you can grow shiitake mushrooms at a fraction of the price of buying them at a farmer's market.

Shiitakes are native to eastern Asia, but they've become popular in America for their nutritional value, meaty texture, and earthy flavor. They work well sautéed or as additions to stir-fries, soups, and pasta.

To grow your own shiitakes, you'll need some logs. Oak, particularly red oak, is ideal. Sugar maple, hornbeam, and hophornbeam work too. American beech also works, but it can be problematic because of its susceptibility to another fungus called Beech Bark Disease.

You may be able to get logs of all these species from a local logger, arborist, or firewood dealer. The sooner after tree felling you can get the log, the better.

Unlike firewood, you'll want the logs unsplit and with the bark as intact as possible. These unsplit logs are commonly called "bolts." They should be about three to four feet long and four to six inches in diameter. That size optimizes growing space for shiitakes while keeping the logs light enough to handle.

Once you have your logs, you need to get the shiitakes in them, a process called inoculation. The edible portion of a mushroom—the cap—is really just its reproductive part. Most of the fungus lives as fungal strands within the log.

To inoculate your logs, you'll need mushroom spawn. You can buy spawn online mixed in with sawdust or compressed into a plug. Use a corded drill to make holes in the bolt 7/16 inch wide and 1.25 inches deep. Start one inch from the bolt's

To grow your own shiitakes, use smaller logs. Red oak is preferred, although other species can work. Photo: Keith Weller, U.S. Department of Agriculture Agricultural Research Service

Although I can't encourage wild mushroom picking, growing your own shiitakes is a safer alternative.
Photo: Yuval Zukerman on Unsplash

end and space the holes three inches apart in rows down the length of the log. You can drill rows around the whole log, but keep three to four inches between them.

You'll need a special tool, available from mushroom farm suppliers, to inject the spawn into the holes. The spawn should be tightly packed in the hole and not quite fill it. Leave about 1/8 inch of space below the log surface.

To hold the spawn in place, apply hot wax to seal each hole. Wax also helps keep the spawn from drying out and reduces cross contamination with wild fungi. Use a food-grade wax like cheese wax or beeswax.

Once your logs have been inoculated, the mushrooms need time to grow. The best place to grow them is in a place with year-round shade and high humidity. A spot beneath some dense conifers in your yard can work well. Behind the north side of buildings like your house can also work. Use shade cloth if needed to provide additional shade.

You'll have to be patient when growing shiitakes. It takes the fungus up to 18 months to colonize the log and start fruiting.

During that time, you may need to pour some water on the log if you get a long dry spell. It's important to keep the log moist to maintain a favorable fungal growing environment.

Mushrooms will appear a few at a time. If you want a lot all at once, you can force the fungus to make mushrooms by "shocking" the log.

You do this by submerging the log in water for 24 hours.

Pull the log from the water and lean it against the side of a building. Monitor the log, and you should soon see mushrooms sprouting all over it. They will usually be ready to harvest seven to ten days after shocking.

Harvest the shiitakes when the cap is still curled and somewhat closed. The gills on the mushroom's underside should be visible. Over-ripe mushrooms flatten out and widen. They're still edible but not as tasty.

While the mushrooms are forming, don't let them freeze. Freezing can stop their growth or give them an unpleasant texture when eaten. Keep rain off them too, as that can make the mushrooms soggy.

You can shock a bolt once every six to eight weeks to encourage fruiting. A productive log can make mushrooms for up to five years.

Peak production happens in the second and third year. A typical log will produce three to four pounds of fresh mushrooms over its usable life.

Even though you're growing shii-takes, still read up on mushroom identification. Cross-contamination with other fungi can happen. The shiitake can survive and produce mushrooms when other mushrooms are present, but you want to make sure you only harvest the shiitakes and not the wild (and potentially poisonous) other mushrooms that may appear.

MAKE MAPLE SYRUP

Like growing your own mush-rooms, making maple syrup is an-other way to blend foraging and farming. And you don't need a forest to do it. A single large maple tree in your yard can yield enough sap to make several batches.

In theory, just about any kind of maple tree can be tapped, but some kinds produce more and sweeter sap than others. Not surprisingly, the aptly named sugar maple is the traditional choice because of its sap's high sugar content. That said, both red and silver maples also work for making syrup.

Maples have a big range, but not everyone with a maple tree can tap it for sap. The climate where you live makes a big difference in whether

Sugar maples are the go-to trees for maple syrup because of their sap's high sugar content. Identify sugar maple leaves by looking for smooth leaf edges and a distinct, five-lobed shape. Photo: Pixabay

you can make your own syrup.

Sap only runs in late winter, and only under specific weather conditions. Good sap flow requires cold, sub-freezing nights paired with warmer, above-freezing days.

To make your own syrup, first you have to get sap, then boil it down. For a first attempt, you'll need:

- A tree to tap
- Galvanized steel bucket with a cover
- Cordless drill
- Spout
- One or two clean gallon jugs for sap storage
- Pan with high sides
- Turkey fryer
- Candy thermometer
- Food-approved filter
- Jars for finished syrup

You can get all these products through a maple supply store. Many are also available through general online retailers as well.

For the first tree you tap, if you have a choice, choose a large, open-grown sugar maple close to your home. Open-grown trees with big canopies produce more sap, and they have higher sugar content. Make sure the tree you pick is at least ten inches across at chest height.

To tap your tree, use a 7/16 inch drill bit to drill two inches into the tree at a slight upward angle. Do this on a day when it's above freezing at the start of sap season. That's usually sometime in February, though it varies depending on where you live. Pick a tap spot free of scars, wounds, and rot.

You'll know you have a good spot if the shavings coming off your drill are lightly colored. If they're dark, abandon that hole and try a different spot.

Tapping a maple for sap doesn't harm the tree. A fresh tap hole (left) will heal over in about a year (right). Trees more than ten inches across can be tapped every year. Position new tap holes at least six inches away from those drilled the previous year. Author photos

Unless you're setting up a commercial syrup operation, the old-fashioned approach of hanging a bucket on a maple tap is the best way to collect sap for home use. Photo: National Park Service

The hole's height is up to you. Position it so your bucket is off the ground and accessible for collection.

Once you've drilled into the tree, gently tap the spout into it. When seated properly, the spout will support the bucket all by itself. Hang the bucket on the spout and cover the top.

Check the bucket daily during sap season, which can run through the end of March. A single tap hole can produce ten gallons of sap, and a big yard tree may yield more.

It's important to collect and process the sap quickly, because bacteria love its blend of sugar and water. Plan to boil your sap into syrup at least once a week throughout tap season to keep it from spoiling.

At the end of sap season, remove your bucket and tap from the tree. The tree will regrow over the tap wound on its own.

In future years, make your new tap hole at least six inches away from your previous one to give the tree space to heal. You can tap healthy maple trees larger than ten inches across every year without harming them.

Now that you have some sap, it's time to start boiling. Maple sap is about two percent sugar, but final maple syrup is 66-67 percent sugar.

That percentage is critical. Any lower, and the syrup will mold. But go higher, and it will crystallize.

The way you get to that magic percentage is by boiling off some of the water. If you're making syrup for your own use, you can boil using a turkey fryer and stovetop.

Use the turkey fryer for most of the boiling. Making syrup throws off a lot of steam. You don't want all that moisture in your house.

When the sap thickens, transfer it to a stovetop pan with high sides for greater control. When boiling, always keep at least a couple inches of liquid in the pan to stop the syrup from scorching.

Speed matters in boiling. The faster you boil, the lighter your final syrup will be in both color and flavor. Slow boiling makes darker syrup with a stronger maple flavor.

To know when your syrup is done, you'll need a candy thermometer that can read more than 200 degrees Fahrenheit. You're looking for the final temperature to be 219 degrees.

Once the syrup gets to temperature, put it in containers. Either bottles or jars can work as long as they can withstand the high temperature.

Pass the hot syrup through a food-grade filter before putting it in containers. Refrigerate the syrup right after bottling to let it cool.

If you bottled properly, you won't have to refrigerate unopened containers, and the syrup will keep for more than a year.

Once you open a bottle, keep it refrigerated. Opened, refrigerated syrup will last up to six months.

How much syrup can you expect from one tree? Sugar content varies, but in general it takes forty gallons of sap to make one gallon of syrup. Based on that, one large tree may net you a quart of maple syrup over the course of sap season.

A quart might be enough to last you a year. But if you love maple syrup as much as I do, you'll want to tap a few more trees. It actually makes boiling easier if you have more sap to work with. When you only have sap from one tree, you have so little liquid left at the end that it's easy to go from syrup to burned-on mess. If you start with more sap, you lower the chances of ruining your hard work—and your kitchenware.

Maple syrup is graded on its color. Lighter-color syrup has milder flavor and works best for pancakes. Darker syrup has stronger flavor and is preferred for baking. Photo: Nadine Primeau on Unsplash

Chapter 9

BEYOND THE FIVE

Is that all, or is there more besides? ... For my own part, I declare I know nothing whatever about it. But to look at the stars always makes me dream.
– Vincent Van Gogh

As children, we learn that we have five senses. Like many other things we learn as kids, this seemingly obvious fact turns out to be wrong.

Scientists disagree about how many senses we have, but the consensus is that the number is more than five. Researchers have identified as many as 21 senses in humans. Many of them are internal senses that give us cues about our body, like our abilities to feel hungry, thirsty, or tired.

Internal senses aren't much help for observing nature. But along with these internal senses, we do have external senses beyond the usual five that can deepen our connection with the outdoors.

Often we don't realize we have these senses, let alone give ourselves practice with them. The result? Even if we hone our five major senses, we still don't get the full sensory experience outside that we could have.

This chapter will fix that. We'll explore three senses that together can take an ordinary visit to nature and elevate it into an experience that lingers with you for a lifetime.

SENSE OF BALANCE

Let's do a simple experiment. Close your eyes. Now raise one hand.

Where is your hand? Can you tell its location without looking?

Of course you can. You can contort your body into all kinds of positions, yet you never forget what position you're in. That's because you have a sense called "proprioception." It's more simply called "body sense."

Body sense is the awareness of your body's orientation in space. You don't need any of your other five senses to be aware of it. It is its own sense.

Awareness of your body's position may not seem useful for observing nature. But it is, because focusing on your body sense will improve an important skill for exploring the outdoors: your balance.

Maintaining your balance is all about recognizing your body's position in space. When perched on a narrow log or steep slope, it's your awareness of your body's orientation that keeps you upright.

The challenge is that because body sense is so instinctual, we forget about it. It succumbs to sensory numbness just like our more well known senses do. That's a problem, because body positioning and balance are keys to walking efficiently and with minimal strain.

Most of us are horrible walkers. Considering it's something we've been doing almost all our lives, we're surprisingly bad at it.

Watch people walking along a sidewalk sometime. You'll see what I mean. We don't walk upright. We tend to lean forward with our head out farther than our hips. This bending results in lower back pain.

Our legs constantly strive to keep up with our weight, but they can't. In their desperate effort, our legs shove hard off the ground with each step, using the calf muscles to propel the legs forward rather than the larger and stronger thighs.

Our eyes watch not the horizon but the ground immediately in front of us. Even if we don't run into anyone or walk into traffic, we still miss nearly everything going on around us.

Adjusting the way you walk can help you move more confidently and with less strain on your lower body. At the same time, it can help you observe more.

To start, make a conscious effort to walk truly upright. Keep your torso and head aligned over your hips, not leaning out past them. Aligning your body this way will reduce strain on your lower back.

The uneven terrain of a backcountry hike will force you to pay greater attention to your balance and help you improve it. Photo: Phil Aicken on Unsplash

Another way to hone your body sense is to don a blindfold, then take a walk in the woods.

I realize that sounds dangerous. Won't you walk into a tree or trip over a rock?

Not necessarily. Instead of literally walking blind, start by tying a hundred feet of string through the woods. When you put on the blindfold, hold the string in one hand to guide you. As long as you hold the string, you'll know you're on course.

Blindfolded walking is an excellent partner activity. Set up a course for your partner without them watching, then have them walk it. Let them do the same for you in a different spot.

Blocking your sight with a blindfold will force you to pay closer attention to your other senses, especially your body sense. Photo: Valentin Fernandez on Unsplash

Keep in mind that blindfolded walking isn't a race. You aren't trying to see which partner can get to the other end of their string first. This is a practice exercise for your balance. Without your eyes, you'll need to rely on your less-practiced body sense to guide you. Let it. Move slowly. Focus on walking technique. Go barefoot if you feel comfortable doing so. That will give you even more sensitivity to the ground and help you feel around obstacles.

Blindfolded walking is useful for more than improving your balance. We're such visual creatures that we often ignore our other senses and rely purely on sight. When your sight goes away, you may find that your other senses become sharpened. You'll hear more, and your sense of touch will become more sensitive.

But here's the trick: your other senses haven't become sharper. They were always that strong. You just weren't paying attention to them. Blindfolded walking forces you to do so. In that way, blindfolded walking is not only good balance practice, but a superb way to build your awareness of your other senses too.

Another way to practice your sense of balance is on a stand-up paddleboard, or SUP. Start with sitting or kneeling and work your way to standing. Inflatable models are relatively inexpensive and easy to transport. Many outfitters also rent SUPs if you want to try one before purchasing. Photo: Paddle North on Unsplash

Instead of shoving off the ground with each step, lift your foot gently using your thigh. Keep your eyes on the horizon, and rely on your feet to tell you the lay of the land right around you.

You can practice this walking style anywhere, but practicing off-trail in nature is especially useful. It will force your sense of balance to work harder than it's used to. Your body will need to adjust to the uneven terrain and potential tripping hazards.

The more you walk deliberately in places like these, the smoother and more confident a walker you'll become. In return, you'll find your endurance improves not because of increased lung capacity, but because each step uses less energy and puts less strain on your muscles.

SENSE OF TIME

What is the oldest clock? The clock as we know it dates back nearly a thousand years to medieval Europe, where Christian monks used early clocks to call the faithful to prayer. Candle clocks, which measure time according to the rate a candle burns, date back to 500 AD in China. In 250 BC, the Greeks used water clocks, which tracked the accumulation of water in a vessel. And the ancient Egyptians built obelisks—predecessors to sundials—as far back as 3,500 BC.

Yet none of these are the oldest clocks in the world. Because there is another clock, a natural clock, inside us.

Biologists have discovered that life, whether human, animal, plant, or even bacteria, have mechanisms within their cells that track the passage of time over a 24-hour day.

These internal clocks maintain this cycle even deprived of outside stimulation. Experiments where people have lived in caves or windowless apartments for weeks at a time show that they continue to wake and sleep on close to a 24-hour cycle.

But close isn't perfect. We still need outside input to maintain our daily rhythm—what you may have heard called a "circadian" rhythm.

The input we need is light.

For nearly all the time life on Earth has existed, the only source of light has been the sun. The world brightened in the morning and darkened at night.

And for nearly all of human history, we set our daily patterns based on that light. We rose with the dawn and slept with the dusk. This is time as a natural force.

But we no longer have time as a natural force. With the rise of electricity, we can keep our world bright all the way through the night.

I still recall my first visit to Times Square in New York City. It was in early December well after sunset, yet it was as bright as noon.

All this artificial light diverts our sense of time off its natural track. Instead of day and night, we see time as a construct of hours, minutes, and seconds.

But these units are human creations the same way the light bulb is. They combine with artificial light to make time almost irrelevant.

The problem, of course, is that it is relevant. Our circadian rhythm still seeks that 24-hour equilibrium, but it can't find it. We extend our day into the night using artificial light, and it tricks the brain into thinking the day is longer than it is.

Scientists have a fancy term for this: circadian desynchrony. You can think of it in a simpler word: jetlag.

If you've ever taken a long flight, you know the sensation of jetlag. You cross several time zones, and your body becomes confused about what time it actually is.

The brain gets confused because its built-in 24-hour clock is not in sync with the expected amount of light. It expects the time to be, say,

Modern lighting is incredible, no doubt about it. But it also messes with our internal sense of time.
Photo: Pawel Nolbert on Unsplash

A longer-term way to reconnect with your natural sense of time is to track a tree using a photo point.

Photo points are places where you take a picture from the same location time and time again. For example, you might take a picture of a tree in your yard or local park from the same spot every day for a year. At the end, you can stitch those photos together into a short movie. In the space of a few seconds, you'll be able to watch the tree grow new leaves, have them change color, and finally drop them for the winter.

Key to photo points is taking them from the same spot in the same way every time. Choose a location that will be easy to remember. A park bench or other outdoor structure helps a lot with this. Take the photo at the same time each day, and use the same camera settings. Note the zoom on your camera so the tree takes up the same amount of space in each photo.

Photo points can help you observe lots of slow-moving changes in nature, not just trees. Time-lapse videos of grass growing or flowers blooming are good examples.

Another way to track a tree is to measure the girth it adds to its trunk.

Any flexible tape measure can work to record a tree's circumference. Simply wrap it around the trunk at chest height and look for the measurement where the tape overlaps itself. Record that number year after year, and you'll see for yourself that trees really are living, growing things.

Taking photos of the same tree over time can reveal how plants change. I photographed this massive white oak in February (left) and again in June (right). Apart from the obvious difference from the addition of leaves, the June photo revealed that the tree lost a big limb sometime during the spring. You can see it lying on the ground to the left of the tree in the June photo. Author photos

Common jetlag symptoms: tiredness, headache, and difficulty sleeping. Sound familiar, even though you haven't traveled? Modern living puts us in a constant jetlag state. Photo: Abbie Bernet on Unsplash

2:00 in the afternoon, but based on the amount of light outside, it's actually 7:00 at night.

The consequences, as any experienced traveler can tell you, include tiredness, insomnia, headache, difficulty focusing, and even mild depression.

There is no medical treatment for jetlag. The only way to cure it is to spend some time in the new day/night cycle of your destination. Your internal clock will gradually adjust to that input and help you recover.

Why do I tell you all this? Because you're suffering from jetlag right now. Even if you've never stepped on a plane in your life, you still have jetlag.

Your body's natural sense of time is at war with the human construct of it. In gaining the power to stay up late, we have made it harder for our internal clocks to keep up.

Before, these clocks could predictably assess how much daylight they had to work with. Now, there is no such predictability.

As a result, the same confusion that occurs from jetlag hits us at home, and its effects on our bodies and minds are identical. Worse, the chronic nature of this jetlag can lead to increased risks of digestive disorders and heart disease.

I'm not saying you need to throw away your clocks and light bulbs. I'm not saying you need to go to bed at sunset and wake at dawn. But I want you to realize there is a cost to

Waking up and going to bed with the sun for a couple days on a camping trip is the best way to reset your internal clock. Photo: Kevin Ianeselli on Unsplash

surrounding ourselves with artificial light and to staying up late with lights blazing around us.

If you want to overcome your jetlag, the best way to do it is to spend a night or two outdoors. Don't bring a watch. Keep your phone and any artificial lights off.

Camping gives your internal clock a chance to reset by aligning it with the external light signals it expects. Just like spending time in a new time zone, this outdoor visit will realign your internal clock. Even when you return to the glaring lights of civilization, you'll likely find that you fall asleep faster and feel more energized than before you left.

If you can't spend a weekend in the woods, you can get closer to that reset with a few hours outside.

When you engage in Deep Nature Observation, don't watch the time. The longer you spend in nature this way, separated from the human construct of time, the more in tune you'll become with nature's time— and with your own internal clock as well.

SENSE OF WONDER

Of all the senses I've talked about in this book, none is perhaps more important, nor more in danger, than this last one: our sense of wonder.

I realize that may sound like I'm getting all new age-y on you. But the very fact that a "sense of wonder" sounds like something that isn't a real sense is a sign that something is wrong in our society.

Why? Because while we share

every other sense in this book with animals, the sense of wonder is unique to humans. I would go so far as to say that our sense of wonder is one of the things that makes us human.

What is the sense of wonder? It's the ability to experience connection and meaning beyond the self and those of our family group.

Other animals do not have this capacity. To be sure, many animals form family bonds or herds. Some animals even grieve when a mate or child dies.

But animals do not wonder. They do not concern themselves beyond their immediate surroundings or the members of their herd.

Pets come closest in that they transfer their feelings of family affection from their own species to another—humans. Yet even with pets, that's simply a shifting of family identity.

Apart from being a uniquely human sense, the sense of wonder is, I would argue, our most powerful sense. It's the sense that inspires awe and empathy. It's the source of our imagination and creativity. And it's the sense that inspires us to dream, learn, and pursue a better world not only for ourselves but for all people now living and those yet to come.

This sense is in deeply short supply in modern culture. Far from connecting us, the Internet and social media in many ways have created a cacophony of voices

Our abilities to think beyond our immediate surroundings and experience connection with the broader world are fundamental parts of what make us human. Photo: NASA

concerned only with speaking, not listening. We blast our thoughts out into the digital void, but are we actually hearing the conversation? Increasingly, we are not.

Our sensory numbness is also to blame. We believe we have "seen it all before," and thus we have no reason to learn or grow, whether as individuals or as society.

The truth is we have seen almost nothing, and we know even less.

The consequences of losing our sense of wonder are devastating. Without wonder, we see only ourselves, and thus we become the only ones who matter.

We see the loss of wonder in our politics, where there is no longer

When we close ourselves off to nature by thinking we have "seen it all before," we miss out on the chance to let nature inspire us, to build our empathy, gratitude, and joy. Photo: Jonny Auh on Unsplash

space for compromise, common ground, or even hearing other points of view. Political opponents are not merely wrong. They're stupid, crazy, or evil.

We see the loss of wonder in our treatment of nature. Too many of us no longer care about the diversity of life we share Earth with. We happily destroy the last of an endangered animal's habitat because it's "jobs versus the environment." We refuse to accept the reality of climate change because it might require us to act differently and care for something besides ourselves.

Worst of all, we see the loss of wonder in the way we treat other people. Too many of us fear the Other—those who have a different skin, pray to a different God, or have a different definition of love. Instead of seeing them as people, each as complex as we are, we stereotype them and treat them as scapegoats—if not outright villains.

I'm not one to stand on soapboxes, but this soapbox is worth standing on. Deep Nature Observation is a way to connect with nature and improve your own health, yes. But writ large, I believe it's also a way we can start to heal some of the divisions in our society. Why? Because nature has the ability to invoke wonder on a level that almost nothing else can.

In fact, when psychologists researched how feelings of awe affect us, they chose a forest as the location to induce awe in the people they studied.

Do you know what those researchers found? Feelings of awe and wonder have remarkable power.

After experiencing a sense of wonder, people thought less about themselves and more about others. They became more generous. They felt less entitled. They became friendlier and more helpful. And they became more socially accepting of others.[1]

As powerful as feelings of awe and wonder are, actually causing them can be challenging. You have to be willing to acknowledge your own weakness and limitations. That's hard to do in a cynical, self-centered social media bubble culture that rewards big egos and blustery overconfidence.

But we need to find ways to do it, each of us. I don't think it's stretching to say that society depends on it.

One way to develop your sense of wonder is to travel. It's hard to walk among 350-foot redwoods with trunks wider than cars and not feel awe. It's similarly difficult when gazing upon the Grand Canyon, Angel Falls, the Himalaya Mountains, or the Nordic fjords.

Of course, not all of us can afford to visit these places. Certainly not as often as we'd like to strengthen our sense of wonder.

That's why I believe Deep Nature Observation is such an important skill. Deep Nature Observation calls on us to see that same awe-inspiring beauty and complexity right in front of us, in the parks and paths we visit all the time. To see the intricate structure of an aster, hear

To walk among giants like this sequoia is to remember that for all our brainpower, we are tiny creatures in a very big universe. Photo: National Park Service

the haunting beauty of the hermit thrush, taste the pungent flavor of a wild leek.

Use what you've learned these past six chapters. Use it to improve your hikes, hunts, and fishing trips. Use it to improve your walks in your local park. Use it to improve your health and boost your mood.

But above all, use it to remind yourself that there is a world out there more complex than you could ever understand. Use it, so that you will never lose your sense of wonder, but instead strengthen it for the good of all.

The researchers in the awe experiment defined awe as "that sense of wonder we feel in the presence of something vast that transcends our understanding of the world." There isn't much out there more vast than space. When it comes to inducing awe, space is the place.

To experience the vastness of space, get away from city lights. Artificial light blocks most stars. To see the dimmest stars, you need as dark a sky as possible. If you can, go on a clear night with no moon. Moonlight also blocks stars.

Find a field and lie down. You can lie on a blanket if you want, or just lie in the grass and feel the Earth beneath you.

Now look up.

Stay in that position at least half an hour. Recall from the Sight chapter that your eyes need time to adjust to the dark. The longer you lie there, with starlight your only source of illumination, the more of the sky you'll see.

If you've never really seen the night sky before, this experience will almost certainly induce awe. The night sky you're used to seeing in your city contains only a few of the brightest stars. When you realize how many stars there are—and then how infinitely more are beyond your sight—you'll inevitably feel that vast presence that is awe.

When you reach that point, don't stop watching the sky. Keep going, and something truly magical may happen. You may switch from feeling small to feeling large. Not large in the sense of yourself or your ego, but large as in a connection to that vastness of space.

In effect, your sense of self becomes so small that you stop thinking about yourself at all. For that brief time, you become one with the stars and the grass and this beautiful planet you're lucky enough to live on. Ironically, after spending a section on developing a sense of time, you may find that your sense of time vanishes. In a way it will almost feel like sleep, like dreaming, yet you'll remain wide awake.

Your senses may take on a hyper focus. You'll hear sounds you never heard, spot flickers of bats overhead, and feel animals moving around you with no fear of your presence. In that moment, you'll have made a true connection with the universe—a oneness I cannot describe scientifically, but only in terms of transcendence.

At some point, I cannot say exactly when, that realization will hit you. Your conscious mind will awaken and realize something has happened. At that point the spell will break, and you'll be back in your body, back in your own head, aware of your own sensations.

When that happens, get up and head inside for the night. But as you fall asleep, that feeling of connection will linger. That is awe. That is wonder.

That is the hope of this world.

Chapter 10

OUTDOOR PHOTOGRAPHY

When words become unclear, I shall focus with photographs. When images become inadequate, I shall be content with silence.
— Ansel Adams

In the past six chapters, we focused on skills to hone your individual senses. But your senses don't work independently of one another. Three-dimensional listening uses vision to assess distance. Taste relies on smell to enhance flavors. When we combine our senses, we get an even richer outdoor experience.

That's why I've included these last few chapters. The topics in these chapters apply and blend the sensory skills you've learned so far to create deep, long-lasting outdoor memories.

We'll start with one of the most popular forms of outdoor recreation: nature photography.

Thanks to advances in digital cameras, taking good nature photos has never been easier. Even basic cameras and smartphones now come with features like autofocus and camera shake compensation. Large memory cards let you take thousands of photos and not worry about the cost of film.

And trust me, when you take na-ture photos, most of your photos will be terrible. It comes with the territory. I can't tell you how many thousands of photos I've deleted where the tree leaves are perfectly crisp, and the warbler just behind them is blurry.

As easy as taking good photos has become, that doesn't mean all the skill has gone out of it. Quite the opposite. Since everyone can take good nature photos, the quality demanded for great ones has similarly gone up.

What separates these great photos—and photographers—from normal pictures? It isn't equipment. Sure, there are advantages to a high-powered zoom lens, but you can still take amazing pictures without one.

No, the real separation is observational skill—the very skill you've been honing all through this book.

Great nature photographers are Deep Nature Observation masters. They know exactly when and where to be. They have the patience to wait for the right moment. And they

You'll get better results in your nature photos if you go out early in the morning or late in the evening. I took these two shots of the same location with the same camera settings. The only difference? I shot the left photo at 9:00 AM and the right photo at 2:00 PM. The afternoon shot is full of harsh shadows and washed out tones. By contrast, the morning shot has more even light, yielding sharper textures and richer colors. Author photos

have an awareness of all their senses that let them frame each shot in an unexpected yet beautiful way.

You can gain these skills too. We'll start with an overview of nature photography basics, then delve into particulars for capturing specific, hard-to-photograph subjects.

BASICS OF GREAT NATURE PHOTOGRAPHY

Of all your senses, an awareness of light is the most important when taking pictures in the great outdoors. You're not in a portrait studio where you have direct control over light levels. You're counting on sunlight, and the amount and quality of that light will change depending on season, weather, and time of day.

Camera settings can accommodate some of these differences, but they can't turn poor light into good light. Professional nature photographers can instantly judge both the amount and quality of light in the spot where they're shooting. To improve your nature photography, develop a similar awareness.

In general, the best light for nature photos comes early in the morning and late in the evening. The sun is lower at those times. With that lower height comes longer light rays that give deeper colors. By contrast, photos taken in the middle of the day tend to look washed out and faded.

Along the same lines, don't fear cloudy weather. You might think clouds would mean less light, but they help outdoor shots a lot. Clouds even out sunlight and eliminate harsh shadows. They're especially useful when taking pictures in forests because you won't have to worry about trees throwing big shadows across your photos. Clouds also reduce glare when taking pictures of objects out in the open, like flowers in a meadow.

Watch your own shadow too. You'll typically want the sun behind you or to the side when photographing outside. Positioning that way avoids glare and gives deeper colors. Unfortunately, that position also means your shadow can easily creep into your photos.

Beyond light, think about what you're taking a picture of. I don't just mean your subject. I mean everything around it. Photographers call this "framing" and "composition." You can think of it more simply as the answer to one question: how much background do you want to show?

In some cases, you'll want to minimize background and fill the picture with your subject. Other times, that background can give important context.

Wildlife photos, in particular, benefit from some background. The background gives information about where the animal lives and what it's doing.

As best you can, get level with your subject. Photographing wildflowers? Get on your knees or even down on your belly. Want a close-up of an autumn leaf? Choose one that's hanging low enough that you can position the camera across from it rather than below.

Above all, don't be afraid to take a "bad" photo. With digital cameras, the cost of a missed shot is zero.

If you aren't sure if a shot will turn out, take it anyway. Then adjust your camera settings a little and try again. Keep taking photos until you're satisfied (or, in the case

I could have gone for an extreme close-up on this house wren, but instead I kept more background to show where it lives—a spiny hawthorn shrub that protects it from predators. Author photo

of wildlife photography, until your subject leaves).

Who cares if you delete ninety-nine out of a hundred photos? The one you keep is worth the effort.

BIRDS

Although I enjoy taking pictures of just about anything in nature, birds are my favorite subjects. With their bombastic colors and surprising personalities, they can make wonderful photographs.

They can also be colossal pains.

Many parks and nature preserves set up nest boxes to help birds like these tree swallows. The areas around these boxes can provide excellent photography opportunities, especially in spring. Just make sure to give the birds plenty of space so you don't disturb their nesting. Author photo

When you think about it, birds are just about the hardest natural subjects to photograph. They're small, so you need to get close to see detail. But when you get close, they fly away.

Even if they do stick around, birds are always moving. Feeding, twitching, preening, singing...they absolutely cannot sit still.

How do you overcome these difficulties and snag a bird shot you'll be proud to show off? It takes patience, equipment, and technique, but you can do it.

Let's start with equipment. It really helps if you have either a camera with a high zoom or one with interchangeable lenses. That will overcome the need to get right in the bird's face. Look for telephoto lenses of at least 350mm.

If you can get a little higher, 450 or even 500mm will let you take pictures from farther away. I use a 350mm telephoto, and there are plenty of times I wish I had just that little bit more magnification. Those times usually occur when I take one step too close to a bird and spook it just when I thought I had it large enough in my frame.

On cameras without interchangeable lenses, take care that you only use the "optical" zoom, not the "digital" one. Optical zoom uses the glass inside the lens to magnify the image. Maxing optical zoom won't affect image quality as long as you have adequate light.

By contrast, digital zoom crops your photo to create the appearance of greater zoom. Instead of a crisp image, your final picture will look grainy. It may appear fine on your phone screen or camera viewfinder, but it will turn out fuzzy or pixelated when blown up on a monitor or printed.

What do you do if you don't have a camera with a big zoom or telephoto lens? Grab your binoculars or a spotting scope. In a technique known as "digiscoping," you line up your camera's lens with one of the eyepieces on your binoculars or scope. The binoculars provide the magnification instead of a fancy camera lens.

The trick to digiscoping is keeping everything steady. The slightest wobble can shift the camera and binoculars out of alignment and result in blurry photos or missed shots.

For best results, mount your scope or binoculars on a tripod. If you have a second tripod, attach your camera to it, line up the lens with the scope, and trigger the camera with a remote shutter. If you don't have a second tripod and need to hold the camera yourself, then only shoot in well-lit conditions so you can use a short shutter speed.

As with any outdoor photography, light will make or break your digiscope shots. Avoid using your camera's zoom, because it will make you lose light and cause dark photos. If you have issues with vignetting (where the image doesn't fill the camera's field of view, resulting in black edges), crop the image later

A telephoto lens will make bird photography easier, but you can use other methods, like digiscoping or setting up a birdfeeder. Photo: Dima Solomin on Unsplash

rather than zooming in while taking the photo.

Strange shadows in your photos are another common problem when digiscoping. To combat them, make sure the camera lens and scope eyepiece align as close as possible. That will avoid extra light leaking in, which causes the shadows.

Depending on the camera and scope you use, you may be able to get an adapter that will connect the two. Adapters exist for smartphones too, so check those out if you want to use your phone to take bird photos.

If digiscoping sounds too complicated, another way to take bird photographs is to use a hunting blind. Here's what you do. Put a birdfeeder near a bush in your yard, then set up a portable ground blind nearby. Get in the blind with your

Keep taking bird photos even after you think you have a good shot. I took a decent photo of a gray catbird (left), but a few seconds later the bird sang. Since I was still taking pictures, I landed a more dynamic shot of the bird with its mouth wide open (right). Author photos

camera or smartphone and wait quietly.

Birds will come to the feeder. While they wait for their turn, they'll hang out in the bush for cover. With you hidden in the blind, you can poke your camera or smartphone lens out through the blind without the birds noticing you.

This method lets you get mere feet away from birds—close enough to take pictures even without a big zoom. It also has the advantage of shooting at the same height as the birds, which will result in more dramatic images.

Whatever equipment you use, applying some general photography tips will get you better bird shots. Taking the photo so the bird is slightly off-center, for instance, will result in a more interesting photograph. Also make sure at least one of the bird's eyes is facing you and in focus. The eye will give the bird

personality, much like a human face.

Finally, perhaps the most important piece of advice when photographing birds is to keep taking pictures even after you think you have a good shot. As I said, birds are always moving. If you keep taking photos, you may by chance get an especially interesting one, like one where the bird is singing or eating. These action shots are much more dynamic than photos of a bird just sitting on a branch.

MACROPHOTOGRAPHY: UP CLOSE AND PERSONAL

From long-distance bird shots, let's go the other way: getting really close to your subject. Macrophotography means taking pictures of small objects—insects and flowers are good examples—so the final image is larger than life size. Think of it as the photo equivalent of using your hand lens from the Sight chapter.

You don't need fancy equipment to take macro photos. Most modern cameras have a "macro" mode built in. The settings in that mode help the camera focus on objects very close to the camera lens. Turn on that mode, get close to your subject, and you can take good, detailed photos.

That doesn't mean all macro shots are simple. When taking close-ups, pay attention to what your camera is focusing on. I've found with macro that my camera often focuses too precisely. When shooting a flower, for instance, it will focus on one petal and leave the rest of the flower blurry. That variation can result in some arty shots if controlled well, but in most cases I want the whole flower in focus.

To get around that issue, adjust your aperture to a smaller opening—a "high f-stop" in camera jargon. A high f-stop deepens your field of view and puts more of your subject in focus.

The trade-off is that a smaller opening lets in less light, which means you'll need a longer shutter time. That can cause blurry images from you moving the camera. If your macro shots turn out fuzzy, use a tripod and remote shutter to minimize camera shake.

When photographing insects, the "get in close" part of macro-photography can be hard. Insects often fly away just like birds.

If you have the money, most interchangeable lens cameras can fit a dedicated macro lens designed to let you be farther from the insect yet still get that larger-than-life shot.

I photographed this boxelder bug nymph using a 30mm macro lens. What I love most about macrophotography is its ability to reveal details you would otherwise miss, like the individual hairs on the nymph's back. Author photo

At a more budget-friendly spending level, close-up filters and extension tubes can attach to some cameras and allow for higher magnification.

I've also had luck using my telephoto lens to photograph insects. The key is to find the absolute minimum distance where your lens will focus sharply on a subject. For my telephoto, it's about eight feet. Stand that distance away from the insect and take the picture. Is it professional level? Probably not, but you can still see impressive detail.

SNOWSCAPES

Winter photography can be hard on both you and your camera. When I worked in snowy Syracuse, New York, my boss liked to quip, "There's no such thing as inappropriate weather. There's only inappropriate clothing."

It's a good line, but "appropriate clothing" for upstate New York winters isn't necessarily appropriate for taking pictures. Have you ever tried to use a camera while wearing ski gloves? I have. It doesn't work.

To take pictures in winter, you need to balance warmth with flexibility. You need heavy enough clothing to protect you from the cold, but you also need your fingers mobile enough to work your camera.

To achieve that balance, follow the old maxim of winter hiking: dress in layers. That way you can shed clothes as you move around and warm up or put them back on if you'll be shooting in the same spot for a while.

For gloves, I bring two pairs. I carry a heavy pair for when I'm walking and not using the camera.

Your telephoto lens can sometimes work for macrophotography, such as when you have subjects that will dart away. I photographed this dragonfly with my telephoto lens from about eight feet away. Author photo

Snow shots taken on auto tend to be dark, with the snow a dull gray color (left). To get that pure white look (right), raise the exposure compensation on your camera. Counterintuitive, but it works. Author photos

But I also bring a lighter (though still warm) pair nimble enough to let me operate my camera.

I am on an eternal quest for the lightest, most flexible, yet warmest gloves I can find. For the best winter photography experience, develop a similar habit.

Cold weather puts a beating on your camera too. To protect it, do whatever you can to keep it dry. On snowy days, use a snow or rain cover. A trash bag can work in a pinch.

When you finish shooting, cover the lens and put the camera in a plastic sandwich bag before bringing it into a heated space. That will help prevent the lens from fogging up, which can lead to moisture problems. Do this anytime you take photos in cold weather, not just when it's snowing.

If your camera does get wet, don't wipe it off. That risks pushing water deeper between the camera seams. Instead, wrap a dry towel around the camera when you get inside, then let it sit overnight. The towel should absorb the moisture.

Protect your batteries from the cold too. Cold batteries lose charge faster than warm ones, so expect to run through more battery life in winter than you do other times of the year. Even if you don't usually bring a spare battery, do it in winter. Store it close to your body to keep it warm until you're ready to use it.

Once you've protected you and your camera, how do you take great winter shots? The best advice I have is to raise the exposure compensation on your camera.

That might sound backwards. It seems like it would make an already bright snow scene even brighter, but that isn't what happens.

You see, your camera doesn't know

It was barely flurrying the day I took this photo. By using my telephoto lens and a wide aperture, I created the illusion that I was out in a blizzard. Author photo

you're shooting snow. It just sees a mass of brightness, so it adjusts by lowering the exposure. The result? Dull, gray snow.

To get that brilliant white, freshly fallen look, you need to manually increase the exposure. On my camera, +0.7 works well, but experiment with different exposures to find what works best for your equipment.

Sometimes instead of gray, your camera will give snow a bluish tint. If that happens to you, adjust your white balance. Light reflected off snow can trick your camera's auto white balance into choosing an inappropriate setting. Remember, what you want with snow photography is that crisp white look.

Once you have the snow color right, try swapping in a telephoto lens (at least 200mm, or a high zoom if you have a basic camera). Set your aperture low and your shutter speed as fast as you can manage.

This setup is perfect for capturing snowfall—even if it isn't snowing hard. These settings will put your subject in focus yet blur the snow in front of your lens and behind your subject (a low aperture setting blurs the background more). The result will look like snow is flying past your subject and give your shot an unmistakable winter feel. It can also make snowfall appear heavier than it actually is.

To contrast with all that white, when possible choose a subject that offers a pop of color. Many nature snow scenes look almost black-and-white. Including a subject with a lot of color will liven the image.

Finally, watch where you're walking. You don't want to leave trampled boot prints all over your shot. Think ahead and take your picture while the snow is still undisturbed.

FALL COLORS

When taking fall foliage pictures, color is everything. How can you capture all those brilliant yellows, fiery reds, and ruddy oranges that turn the woods into a giant work of art?

The secret, as in so many things, lies in the timing. Fall colors only last a few weeks.

To make sure you get out at the right time, check with your state or province's forestry bureau. Many of these agencies publish fall foliage maps. Find these maps online, then look for places listed as "near peak." I prefer these areas over "peak" because they have a little green left—one more color to add to the mix.

Time of day matters too. Get out early in the morning or late in the evening. The longer light rays will give deeper colors. By contrast, the more direct sunlight at midday and in the afternoon will wash out the colors and make them bland.

Given this narrow shooting window, plan your fall shots ahead. As you explore nature throughout the year, keep an eye out for forest views and other vistas that could yield a lot of fall color.

When you find these locations, write them down or mark them as waypoints in your phone's GPS.

A bright color, like the red crest on this pileated woodpecker, will contrast with snow photos' often black-and-white appearance and make your picture more interesting. Author photo

Attaching a polarized filter to your camera lens, as I did here, can create exceptionally bold autumn colors. Author photo

That way, when you get that one clear, cool, low-humidity morning perfect for taking photos, you can go directly to that spot and start shooting.

Another way to maximize color? Cheat. Add a polarized filter to the end of your camera lens. These cheap filters help your camera capture fall colors better than it could on its own. They also deepen the blue of the sky and sharpen cloud shapes. These effects are hard to replicate in editing software later, so it's worth using the filter at the time of taking the photo.

You can also cheat by picking up the most beautiful leaves you find as you walk, then arranging them in a beautiful area to create your own perfect shot. No one else needs to know the leaves didn't fall in that specific formation.

Although we typically think of wide open views when photographing fall colors, don't limit yourself to them. Yes, those images are breathtaking, but you can create powerful fall shots at smaller scales. Often these intimate photos can be more beautiful than the color carpet from a mountaintop.

Look for small details, like a single perfect red maple leaf or a leaf midway through its color change. This strategy works especially well for those times you can't get away to the mountains and only have your local street or park trees to photograph.

Finally, seek out water. Water and fall colors combine in many ways. Photograph a stream flowing through a forest to create a beautiful mix of color and motion. Alternately, look for clear ponds and lakes, then photograph them when the sun is low to capture reflections of autumn colors in the water.

SUNSETS

You don't need to wait for fall to photograph amazing color. You can experience those same colors almost every day—at sunset.

Even though sunset happens every day, a spectacular shot takes more than snapping a picture at the right moment. As with any outdoor photography, sunset images demand the right weather.

Choose an evening with some clouds. Whether thin and wispy or thick and heavy, clouds reflect the sunset colors and often take on bolder shades of orange and red than the background sky.

Location matters too. Look for the lowest, flattest horizon you can find. There's a reason so many great sunset photos happen at the beach. The low horizon gives the sun the chance to sink farthest in the sky and throw off its longest, deepest color shades.

As focused as you are on color, think about black too. Many sunset photos include silhouettes to contrast against the sun's colors. A silhouette also supplies context so people looking at your picture can get an idea where you took it. Scout locations and choose one with a silhouette that will suggest where you are, like a palm tree or city skyline.

Now let's talk about camera settings. One of the biggest challenges with sunsets is that the amount of light changes rapidly. To deal with that, take several shots.

Switch your camera to manual mode. Start with the shutter speed at 1/60th of a second and the ISO at 200. Now adjust the aperture setting through several levels. Begin with a low, wide-open aperture and gradually step it up to narrower diameters. Take a photo at each aperture setting.

Next, leave the aperture fixed and adjust your shutter times. Start with a faster shutter speed and work your way to longer ones.

Which shot will be the best will change from sunset to sunset. But by taking several pictures this way, you're likely to get at least one really good one.

Don't accept the first round of photos you take either. Plan to shoot for at least half an hour, until the sun completely goes down. The sky changes a lot as clouds move and

Water adds color, movement, and reflection to both fall leaf and sunset photos. Author photo

the sun lowers. Colors will deepen, and new patterns will emerge. Keep taking photos, then pick the best ones later.

Another tip? Use a zoom or telephoto lens. If using a telephoto, aim for at least 200mm, and more is better. That added magnification will make the sun appear bigger in your photo. Since you'll be shooting for an extended period with some longer shutter times, use a tripod to reduce fatigue and camera shake.

To get the colors right, play with your camera's white balance. As with snowscapes, the shadows and long light lengths of sunsets can trick the auto white balance into choosing the wrong setting. That leads to off colors in your final shot.

Before we leave sunset photography, keep a couple safety pointers in mind. First, you should never look directly at the sun. It can damage your eyes and cause blindness.

Along those lines, don't point your lens—especially your telephoto lens—directly at the sun. The lens will magnify the sun's intensity, which can damage your camera's sensor. To play it safe, position the sun off to one side of your photo rather than shooting directly at it. You should also wait to start taking your sunset photos until the sun has set enough that it has lost all its flaming yellow color and shifted entirely to red.

NIGHT AND STAR PHOTOGRAPHY

Don't pack up your camera after sundown. In the first thirty minutes after sunset, the sun throws a lot of indirect light that can yield deep pink and purple tones in the sky. And once night truly falls, you can take some incredible dark sky shots.

To get the best night photos, you

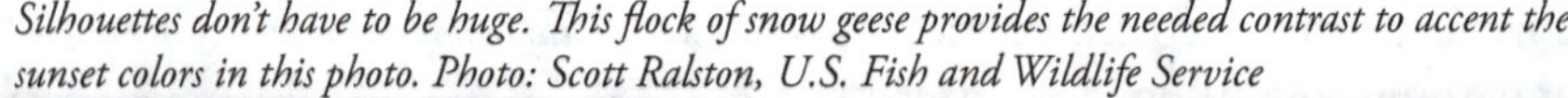

Silhouettes don't have to be huge. This flock of snow geese provides the needed contrast to accent the sunset colors in this photo. Photo: Scott Ralston, U.S. Fish and Wildlife Service

need to get out of the city. Only when you get far away from all those city lights will your eyes—and your camera—be able to truly see the night sky.

Perhaps the most obvious object to photograph in the night sky is the moon. You don't need a fancy telescope to get a good shot of the full moon. Your standard camera lens will work, though if you have a telephoto, use it. Zoom in as far as you can (remember to avoid using digital zoom) and take the shot.

If you're using your camera's default settings, the camera will likely interpret the moon as a ball of white light. You won't see any definition in the moon's surface.

To get that definition, change your camera settings. Instead of shooting in auto, switch to manual. Set the shutter speed to 1/60th of a second, the aperture to f/8, and the ISO to your camera's base level (usually 100). Now take the shot again.

These settings should reduce that bright white glare and reveal the moon's contours. The better magnification you have with your camera, the more of those contours you'll be able to see.

Apart from these settings, weather is key to a good moon photo. You want a clear, cold, low-humidity night. That will reduce atmospheric haze that would otherwise blur the lunar surface.

Winter is often the best season for night photography conditions, so bundle up. If you have access to a higher elevation vantage point, like

Your moon photos will be crisper if you take them on a clear, cold, low-humidity night. I took this shot in mid-November. Author photo

a bare hilltop, that can also make your image crisper.

Don't bother trying to get a clear moon and a clear landscape in the same photo. One or the other will almost always turn out blurry. If you want to pair the two in one photo, take individual photos of each, then combine them in editing software.

The moon isn't the only night sky object you can photograph. If you can get far enough away from all those human lights, you may be able to photograph our galaxy, the Milky Way.

Many people in urban areas never see the Milky Way, because the sky must be very dark with extremely low surface light. That's why a well-done Milky Way shot may become one of your favorite photos.

Unlike the moon, the Milky Way is faint even on dark nights. You'll need every photographic advantage you can muster to take its picture.

Like with the moon, you'll want a dark, clear, and low-humidity night. You'll also want as little moon as possible, because the moon's brightness will obscure the Milky Way. Head out on a new moon for the best chance at a Milky Way shot.

Do whatever you can to reduce the amount of ambient light around your camera. Turn off flashlights, headlamps and car headlights. Bring a flashlight to help you see the camera buttons, but when you take the photo, turn off the flashlight. Remember that a red-light flashlight will help preserve your night vision while shooting.

With all the ambient light removed, the only light reaching your camera should be from the night sky. To shoot the Milky Way,

you need to get as much of that light to your camera as possible.

Shoot in manual and set your aperture as wide open as it goes. Look for the lowest "f/#" option and select it. Set your ISO to 2,000, or higher if your camera can handle it without too much loss of quality. High ISO numbers make it easier to shoot in low light, but they do it at the expense of image precision.

You won't need high zoom for Milky Way pictures, so go with the least amount of zoom you have. That will let in more light.

You'll need a slow shutter speed, but too slow and you'll get motion blur from the Earth's rotation. I'm not joking. Even at 30 seconds,

you'll see blurred lines instead of sharp stars. Limit your shutter speed to 20 seconds or less for the sharpest image. You'll need a tripod to prevent camera shake.

Getting your camera to focus on the Milky Way can be hard. Set the focus to infinity if you have a manual-focus lens. Don't go past infinity! Many manual lenses have this option, but the result won't be as clear as it will be if you shoot at infinity.

If you have an auto-focus lens (as most of you probably do), change the camera's settings to let you manually adjust it. Then zoom in on one star and slowly change the focus until that star is as small as possible.

The way you do this on each camera differs, so look up how to adjust focus manually in your camera's instructions.

If you follow all these steps, you should wind up with a decent shot of the Milky Way. You can check the image quality by adjusting the brightness of your camera's view screen as low as it goes. That will give you a more realistic look at your picture's final appearance.

If the image is too dark, try increasing ISO to 5,000. That may give you that little bit of extra brightness without too much reduction in picture quality.

To get a photo like this one that has both a clear Milky Way and a clear landscape, take two pictures, then composite them together later in editing software. Photo: Casey Horner on Unsplash

Chapter 11

OUTDOOR ART

I think that I shall never see
A poem lovely as a tree.
— Joyce Kilmer

From humanity's earliest days, nature has inspired our creativity. Cavemen painted animals on walls to tell stories of their hunts. Authors like Mary Shelley and William Blake drew on the power and beauty of nature to write their works. Painters like Claude Monet applied their skills to capture the landscapes they lived in.

In turn, artists have often brought attention to environmental causes. In the nineteenth century, the Hudson River School of painters revealed the wanton devastation of unrestricted logging in upstate New York. Their powerful images became a driving force for the creation of the Catskill and Adirondack Preserves, two of the largest protected natural areas in the eastern United States.

Much like outdoor photographers, outdoor artists rely on Deep Nature Observation to craft their pieces. The best outdoor artists find the overlooked details in a landscape or other subject and bring those details to life for viewers.

Even if you don't think you're creative, doing some outdoor art is a superb way to improve your outdoor observation skills. Drawing or writing about nature will force you to pay attention to everything going on around you so you can reflect that experience onto your chosen canvas. You need to see every rock, tree, and cloud. You need to understand what they're doing, which ones have deeper shadows, and how they appear in relation to one another.

With writing, you'll convey senses beyond the visual. What birds do you hear? How does the air smell? What thoughts and emotions does the scene evoke? Outdoor art just may be the most powerful way to blend all your sensory skills together and put them to the ultimate test.

In this chapter I've selected a few outdoor art forms you can try. I encourage you to experiment with them—especially if you think you "can't write" or "can't draw."

The point isn't to become the next Monet. Quality doesn't matter, and no one has to see what you create. Use these media as ways to build deeper connections with the plants, animals, and landforms you find outside. If they inspire your creativity along the way, so much the better.

PLEIN AIR PAINTING

"En plein air" is a French art term. Simply put, it means painting or drawing outside. The idea is to capture a moment in nature as it happens, not the way you remember it or translate it off a photograph.

Painting or drawing outside offers a unique challenge for the artist: movement. The way the light falls when you start painting won't be the way it falls when you finish. The sun or moon will race across the sky, and you'll find yourself racing along with them to catch up.

Painting or drawing "en plein air" means creating your artwork outside. The idea is to capture what you see in nature as it happens. Photo: Dima Novozhilov

Plein air painting requires some extra tools you may not have if you've only ever painted in a studio. You'll need a stand to set your painting on and a box to carry your supplies. Your painting will likely have more green and brown than a typical studio piece, so consider adding those colors to your palette.

Comfort also matters. Bring a portable chair so you can set up in any place where the light is just the way you want it.

Plein air painting has a strong association with landscapes. Big, sweeping vistas scream at the artist to paint them right then and there.

But you don't need grand scenery to make plein air art. Set up beside a stream and trace its flow. Draw a flower growing along a field edge. Study the bark of a sugar maple and record its every plate and groove.

Again, you aren't trying to create "professional" art. You're deepening your appreciation for nature's infinite detail and practicing your ability to observe ever more of it.

When searching for a plein air subject, visit possible sites multiple times and during different weather. Apart from seasonal differences, the angle and quality of light vary and will make a difference in what features and colors stand out.

For a more inspired approach, ditch the planning and rely on chance. Grab your tools, head out early, and start walking or driving in search of a place that catches your attention.

You'll know it when you find it.

It will be the place where something stops you in your tracks. If you find something that powerful, it's worth capturing. Pull out those paints or pencils and have at it.

NATURAL SCULPTURES

You don't need brushes to create art from nature. The outdoors itself provides its own palette of shapes, colors, and textures. You can turn these raw materials into works of natural art.

Perhaps the most well-known outdoor sculpture materials are rocks. The stack of precariously balanced stones has become a cliché symbol for Zen meditation.

Spiritual connections aside, stacking stones provides an exercise not only in creativity, but in Deep Nature Observation. You are literally weighing each stone and deciding where its balance point is so the overall structure can climb ever higher. You'll need all your honed senses of touch and balance to build your tower.

Freshly fallen autumn leaves make another natural sculpture material. In the last chapter I mentioned collecting the best leaves you find and assembling them to create a better fall photo. In that chapter I referred to this practice as "cheating." But in the context of art, it's not cheating at all. It requires having an eye for shape and color and how to arrange them to create something beautiful.

Perhaps you'll drop a leaf into a stream to create a dynamic image. Or you might spread a few leaves out

Stacking stones tests not only your creativity, but your senses of touch and balance. Photo: Wallace Fonseca on Unsplash

fanlike to track the changing colors through the rainbow. Only your creativity limits your possibilities.

When building a natural sculpture, take a few precautions to protect the area you're working in. First, only use building materials that are no longer living. Woven sticks can make a sculpture, but rely on ones that have fallen to the ground rather than ripping live branches off trees. For rocks, avoid using stones from a streambed. Stream rocks shelter fish eggs and aquatic insects, so they play an important role in keeping water bodies healthy. Stones found along a lakeshore, uphill from the stream itself, or along a beach make better stacking options.

Let nature bring out your inner poet. Don't worry. No one's grading you. Photo: Jaz Blakeston-Petch on Unsplash

Finally, make sure you take a picture of your sculpture. By definition, natural sculptures are part of the environment. They're meant to be temporary. Leaves will blow away. Stones will topple. Branches will rot. Your art will vanish with time, but if you save it with a photo, you'll always be able to look back on it and appreciate your creativity.

NATURE POETRY

If the visual arts aren't your thing, try writing about nature instead. Writing a poem can be a fast, creative way to jot down unexpected details about what you observe outside.

For some, writing poetry brings back dark childhood memories. The stern English teacher marks up your hard work with that evil red pen because you didn't follow the rules.

Don't worry. No one will slash apart your work. This nature poem is just for you.

Even if it's just for you, where do you start? That blank page is intimidating. One method I use is to list what I'm sensing.

Try this. Make a chart like the one on the next page. For each sense, fill in something from where you are. For "smell," you might choose a flower. For "feel," you might pick a tree's bark.

Once you have your objects chosen, fill in the description column using the sense you paired with each object. For the bark, you might put "rough, platy, and rigid." The more expressive and unexpected you make these sense descriptions, the better your final poem will be.

You don't have to pick just one object for each sense. Expand the table as big as you want. Maybe there are a bunch of sounds going on. If you're standing beside a stream, you might hear singing birds as well as babbling water.

You won't use all of these observations when writing your poem. That's ok. But the more observations you have, the more inspiration you can draw on later.

As you write down what you sense, other thoughts may jump out at you unbidden: a surprising detail, strong emotion, or connection to memory. Jot these reflections in the chart's last column. They're the stuff great poems are made of—the inspiration no professor can teach. Capture them before they fly from your head like startled birds.

Chart filled out, how do you turn it into a poem? First, narrow your observations to the most compelling ones. You probably found in filling out your chart that one detail or sense stood out more than the rest. Use that detail to start writing.

If you're feeling especially creative—or if you've written poetry before—you may be able to write freeform. Remember, poems don't need to rhyme or follow a certain structure, despite any naysaying from the English teacher in your head.

If freeform is too hard, use a structure. The poem type's rules will help guide your pen. Below are some short structures that work well for nature poems. For each one, I've included the structure and an example of my own. They aren't very good, but that's all right. No one's grading us, remember?

HAIKU

Haiku come from Japan, and they have an eloquent history of communicating short yet powerful observations about nature. They often have a melancholy tone, highlighting both beauty and loss. They have three unrhymed lines that look like this:

1st line – five syllables
2nd line – seven syllables
3rd line – five syllables

As they say on cooking shows, here's one I prepared earlier:

Fields of goldenrod
Turn the world brilliant yellow
Before winter's brown.

TRY THIS – CREATE A POETRY TABLE

Struggling to get over your nature poetry blank page syndrome? Try recreating the chart below on a piece of paper. Fill in something for each sense based on where you are:

Sense	Object	Description	Thoughts, Feelings, and Connections
See			
Hear			
Smell			
Touch			
Taste			

WINDSPARK

Windsparks are one of my favorite nature poems. They're short, and they have a strong pattern that makes them both easy to write yet compelling to read. They look like this. Just fill in the blanks:

1st line – "I dreamed"
2nd line – "I was [something]"
3rd line – [A location]
4th line – [An action]
5th line – [How the action was performed]

Here's an example:

I dreamed
I was an autumn leaf
Clinging to its tree.
I let go
And float home to earth.

ACROSTIC

In acrostics, you write a word vertically down the page. Each line of your poem then starts with one of those letters. You can make each line one word or a longer statement:

Fiery
Iridescence
Rises for
Evening
Flights of
Love
In
Every
Summer

Are there too many poems about fireflies? Not enough, if you ask me. Photo: Tony Phan on Unsplash

LIMERICK

For our last poem type, let's up the difficulty. Limericks combine both rhyming and stressed syllables, which makes them trickier to write.

The effort is worth it though, because limericks are also a lot of fun. They're meant to be humorous, even bawdy.

Limericks have five lines. Lines one, two, and five each have three stressed syllables and rhyme with each other. Lines three and four are shorter. They each only have two stressed syllables, and they rhyme with each other. The first line often follows the pattern, "There once was a [something] named [blank]."

I came up with this example after watching a male robin prance around my front yard like he owned it. He loved to chase away other robins, then stand on this tree stump as if to proclaim himself King of the Yard. This went on for some time, until karma caught up with him:

There once was a robin named Jake,
Who'd whinny so hard he would shake.
He'd swing his big rump,
On that old rotten stump,
'Til he got chased off his throne by a snake.

There are lots of other poem structures. You'll find some easier or more compelling than others. Play around with lots of styles and see what works for you.

Just do me one favor. Don't mark them up with a red pen.

Robins have a way of strutting around the yard like they're the bosses of everything. That sort of pride just begs for a limerick to take them down a peg. Photo: Trac Vu on Unsplash

NATURE JOURNALING

I mentioned nature journaling briefly in Chapter 3 as a way to record your observations in nature. While it isn't as freeform as the other art ideas in this chapter, it can help you attend to and capture details while practicing Deep Nature Observation.

What I enjoy most about nature journaling is that over time, it gives you a vehicle to go beyond observing. The ability to look back through months or years of entries lets you ask questions about your local environment. How has this place changed from one season to another? What about year to year, or decade to decade?

Nature often feels static, but it changes all the time. Trees fall in storms. Flowers bloom and die.

The close observations from nature journaling can help you remember unique experiences outside. Take this red eft I spied on a spring hike. I thought something seemed odd about him, so I started journaling. It took me a minute of careful watching to spot it: the poor little newt is missing an eye. To this day, it's the only one-eyed wild animal I've seen. Yet if I hadn't been journaling and snapped this picture, I'm sure I would have forgotten this unique encounter. Author photo

Streams shift course. You can't track every change, but by recording what you can, you'll capture a tiny fraction of nature's dynamic life.

Nature journaling can take a variety of forms depending on what you're comfortable with. I tend to combine writing and photographs. Many other outdoor lovers use sketches and drawings.

Again, quality doesn't matter. When you see books about nature journaling, they're usually written by professional artists and filled with lifelike renderings of animals and plants you've never heard of.

Don't let the pros intimidate you into thinking you can't nature journal. Your nature journal can be stick figures if that works for you.

You don't need to write down species names or only seek out rare creatures either. Take pictures of chipmunks and other common species. It's all right.

A nature journal isn't a technical document. Like everything else in this chapter, it's simply another way of capturing an outdoor moment as it happens.

When I nature journal, I start with easy information. What's today's date? What time is it? Where am I? What's the weather like?

These questions seem basic, but by writing them down, I accomplish three things. First, I get over the "blank page" fear. I'm already writing before I realize it. Second, a lot of nature revolves around weather. Recording it will help you connect observations later.

Finally, and most importantly, answering these questions puts me in the observation mindset. I make a conscious effort to go beyond the obvious. I could just say the weather is "sunny" or "overcast," but instead I go into more detail. What's the temperature? How about the humidity? What are the clouds doing? Have they changed since this morning?

If you're interested in trying nature journaling, I have a series of four journals called *Young Explorers*. They contain prompts like the questions above to guide you. They're designed for kids, but usable by anyone.

How do you choose what to journal about? Pick whatever catches your attention. You can't talk about everything, so don't. Instead, write about something specific that you find interesting, amusing, or odd. Maybe it's a bird in a tree, a shrub in bloom, or a funny-looking rock. It doesn't matter as long as you're curious about it.

Some nature journal writers avoid reflection and only discuss what happens. But this is a case where I encourage you to let your emotions and musings find their way into your observation. They're part of your experience too, and recording them alongside what you observe will help with recall later. As a bonus, you'll get the well-documented mental health benefits that come with journaling.

Your nature journal can also pose questions you want to dig into later. The most common may be, "What did I see?" Write this next to your sketch of an animal you couldn't identify. When you go inside, use a field guide or online key to figure out what it was.

Identification in the field is overrated. Record the best description you can, then spend your time actually watching and enjoying the cool critter you discovered.

Nature journaling is something anyone can do. It doesn't matter your age, where you live, your ability to identify species, or how little artistic talent you have. Photo: Brett Billings, U.S. Fish and Wildlife Service

Chapter 12

MENTAL HEALTH

To sit in the shade on a fine day, and look upon verdure, is the most perfect refreshment.
– Jane Austen

Throughout this book, I've emphasized the mental health value of Deep Nature Observation. Slowing down and taking time to absorb nature with all your senses has profound benefits for reducing stress and mental health challenges like ADHD, anxiety, and depression.

Why, then, have I included a chapter specifically devoted to mental health? Because as amazing as nature is for improving our mood, other practices also provide mental health benefits. When we combine these methods with Deep Nature Observation, we get something especially powerful.

Now it's worth pointing out that, like any mental health activity, time in nature isn't a cure-all. It doesn't replace consultation with a doctor or medication where needed.

For those with diagnosed mental health disorders, it's important to follow your doctor's and therapist's advice. View time in nature as a supplement to their recommended treatments.

The outdoors are a piece of the therapeutic puzzle, not the solution by itself. Still, in the fight against these disorders, we need every tool we have.

STRESS OR ANXIETY?

We often lump "mental health" into one category, as though all mental health challenges were the same. Consider "stress" and "anxiety." Don't they mean the same thing—that we have a lot to worry about?

No. Stress comes from feeling overloaded—that we have more responsibilities than we have time to deal with. The modern world imposes stress on us as we struggle to balance jobs, relationships, and all the many tasks in life.

Anxiety is different. Anxiety comes from worrying about something beyond its importance or likelihood of happening. It causes stress, but that stress is out of proportion with the actual threat—if the threat even exists.

Understanding this difference is critical, because different mental health techniques apply to each challenge.

If you have stress, simply taking time to walk outside and clear your head may help you relax. But if you suffer from anxiety, "clearing your head" is the last thing you want to do.

Anxiety is like an echo chamber. Give it more space, and it simply grows to fill the gap.

Remember those looping thoughts we talked about earlier? They're the source of a lot of our anxiety. They amplify inside your head, swelling beyond their true importance.

To be sure, time in nature can reduce stress. The science is proven. For this chapter, though, I want to go beyond stress and think about anxiety. Deep Nature Observation can be a tool in addressing anxiety, because it solves anxiety's seemingly paradoxical challenge: the more you "relax," the worse the anxiety gets. Deep Nature Observation addresses that challenge by not clearing your mind, but filling it.

MINDFUL MEDITATION

A branch of meditation aims to achieve this same result to address anxiety. Mindful meditation involves paying attention to something simple, like your breath. Other variations might have you watch a candle, repeat a mantra, or count beads on a rosary.

In all of them, the idea is the same. Instead of letting your mind loop endlessly, you give it something simple to do.

As much as we say we want to relax, our brains want to be active.

Deep Nature Observation can help with anxiety, because it isn't about emptying your mind. Instead, it engages your mind with close attention to nature. Activities that combine multiple senses, like gardening, are especially effective. Photo: Sandie Clarke on Unsplash

They want to *do*. When they can't, they fill the void with anxiety. By giving them a task, no matter how simple, we focus our brains and push away anxiety.

For some, mindful meditation has limits. Anxiety may overwhelm the mind's effort to focus.

Here's where nature can build on this already valuable practice. Try mindful meditation outside. I've found it easier and more effective than in my house.

Outside, my thoughts may wander, but they don't wander into anxiety. Instead, they wander to that bird call I just heard, the rustle of movement in those fallen leaves, and that smell wafting on the breeze. Instead of counting breaths, I explore my surroundings from a seated position.

You don't need much to do mindful meditation outdoors. Leave your phone in your pack, or at least turn it off. If you want to bring a yoga mat you can, but you don't have to.

Outside, find a place where you're unlikely to be disturbed. Go back in the woods off trail a bit, or head to an infrequently visited park or natural area. Your backyard can work if it isn't too noisy.

Sit on the ground with your legs crossed in front of you. Sit up straight, allowing your spine its natural curve.

Don't expect to reach a meditative state right away. Spend a few minutes simply sitting. Take a few deep breaths. Your arrival will have disturbed the animals living nearby.

When practicing mindful meditation in nature, let your attention drift to the sounds you hear. Try to listen without judging. Photo: Steven Cordes on Unsplash

Give them time to calm down right alongside you.

In traditional mindful meditation, you might close your eyes to minimize distraction. Do that for outdoor meditation too, if you like. That will let you concentrate on your other senses, especially your hearing.

Remember the Sound Map? Make one in your head. Note each sound and use your three-dimensional listening to estimate its location. Then relax your ears and take in more sounds.

Focus on each sound one at a time. Explore it. Hear its tonal variations.

Don't worry about what's making the sound or why. You aren't birding. You don't need to concern yourself with species identification. It can simply be enough to go, "Oh,

Returning to the same spot time and again for meditation will train your brain to enter a meditative state any time you go there. This doesn't have to be a place deep in the wilderness either. A park bench away from crowds will work perfectly. Photo: Rafael Sales on Unsplash

that's a different bird from the one I just heard."

Try to listen without judging. Listening is external. Judging is internal. You want to push out internal thoughts and replace them with external sensations. The more you can do that, the harder it will be for those pesky anxieties to find space in your brain.

As animals become more active around you, slowly open your eyes. Keep them in wide-angle vision mode. Scan the landscape in front of you. Again, try to notice without judging. Don't worry about identifying species.

If something catches your attention, follow it. Pay attention to its details as best you can without moving.

When you feel your attention wandering, let it. Release your effort on whatever you were watching and return to wide-angle vision. Your eyes will find something else of interest. Follow that.

At first you may only be able to sit like this for a minute or two. That's ok. Meditation is a skill. Like any skill, it takes practice.

Try doing mindful meditation outdoors once each week. Over time, you may find that you can sit longer, observe deeper, and reach a stronger external connection than you could when you started.

If you have a good experience at one spot, remember that location. The next time you practice outdoor mindful meditation, return there. Do your best to set yourself up the same way you did the last time.

You won't get bored. Quite the opposite. Returning to the same spot may well accelerate your ability to reach that deeper meditative state. Your mind will eventually get in a habit. It will know, subconsciously, that this place is the spot where it stops brooding and lets the outside world fill it for a while.

PROGRESSIVE MUSCLE RELAXATION

Progressive muscle relaxation offers a similar mental health boost as mindful meditation. It's used to treat insomnia, but it can also help those dealing with stress and anxiety.

Similar to meditation, progressive muscle relaxation gives the mind something to focus on beyond those looping thoughts. The idea is to systematically tighten and then relax all the muscles in your body.

The first time you try progressive muscle relaxation, do it in bed. Turn out the lights. If you have a partner, ask them not to be in the room. You want to minimize distractions.

Lie on your bed face-up. Close your eyes. As with mindful meditation, take a few deep breaths to begin the relaxation process.

Start at your toes. Clench them for five or ten seconds, then release the tension. Notice how your body feels when the level of tension changes.

Work your way up your body. From your toes, next tighten and release the muscles in your feet, then your calves, then your thighs. Hit every muscle group. End with your face.

Over time, you'll learn to identify the muscles where your body stores the most tension. Certain muscle groups tense up more when you feel stressed. I store mine in my shoulders. They subconsciously rise when I'm stressed, putting tension in my lower neck and upper back.

Once you know which muscles store tension, notice throughout your day when those muscles become tight. That will signal you that you're becoming stressed.

Hit that stress right at that moment by consciously relaxing those muscle groups. You'll gradually diminish the toll stress wreaks on your body.

When you become comfortable with progressive muscle relaxation inside, take it outdoors. As with mindful meditation, you can bring a yoga mat if you'd rather not lie on

A yoga mat outside can help you practice progressive muscle relaxation without needing to lie on the ground. Photo: Angelina Sarycheva on Unsplash

the ground.

Go through your same muscle relaxation steps you used inside, but now let your senses expand out at the same time. Far from distracting you, nature's sounds and smells will relax you further.

Progressive muscle relaxation can be a practice by itself, but combine it with mindful meditation for even deeper results. When you first reach your spot outdoors, use progressive muscle relaxation to calm your body and focus your mind. It's a useful practice while you wait for wildlife around you to adjust to your presence.

By the time you finish with progressive muscle relaxation, animals will have become more active again. You can then move right into observing them with mindful meditation.

THE FIVE-MINUTE NATURE VACATION

Although longer is better when it comes to nature and health benefits, research has found that as little as five minutes a day can significantly boost your mood. If you don't have the time or privacy to do progressive muscle relaxation in your local park, taking a miniature nature break can give some of the same benefits.

I recommend doing this nature relaxation technique each day on your lunch break. The first step is the hardest. Put your phone in a desk drawer. Now walk outside without it. It may be stressful at first, but if you do this exercise regularly, you'll start to feel liberated from your constant electronic companion.

Once you're outside, it doesn't matter where you are. Even in the

Sitting still with progressive muscle relaxation and mindful meditation will help wildlife get used to your presence, as well as focus your attention. Without intending to, you may find that you hear and see more wildlife than you ever have just wandering the woods. Author photo

The five-minute nature vacation is especially useful for city dwellers, where you may only have a few minutes on your lunch break to reconnect with the outside world. Photo: Jason Krieger on Unsplash

city, nature surrounds you, from the street trees to the wind to the passing birds. They're all nature—even the pigeons.

Find a spot where pedestrians won't run you over. If you're comfortable doing so, close your eyes. Take a deep breath in. Hold it. Release it slowly.

Next, turn your attention to your body. Start your head and move slowly down to your toes. Feel each part of you. What feels tense? When you find those spots, focus on them. Take another deep breath and relax those muscles. Use those progressive relaxation techniques.

Once you've relaxed your body, focus on your surroundings. Keep your eyes closed at first. What do you hear? Traffic, sure, but what else?

Is that a robin singing in a nearby tree? What do you smell? What do you feel? Bring your nature sensing skills to bear in this short moment.

The last step in this mini vacation is to open your eyes. Try not to focus on any one person or object. Instead, let your vision stay blurry. Use your wide-angle vision to take in the city or other landscape around you. Turn your head slowly from side to side, then up and down. What do you notice? Colors? Shapes? What's moving? What isn't?

Take one last deep breath and head inside. You've had a whole mini outdoor vacation in just five minutes. Not bad. You might just feel so good that you'll leave that annoying phone in the drawer the rest of the afternoon.

A walking meditation combines the mental relaxation of meditation with the physical stimulation of movement. It provides yet another way to focus on the moment rather than worrying about the future. Photo: Pixabay

WALKING MEDITATION

As effective as mindful meditation and progressive muscle relaxation are, sometimes nervous energy demands a physical outlet. Walking meditations combine mental relaxation with the physical stimulation of movement.

To do a walking meditation, find an area outdoors with level ground. You don't need a lot of space, just enough to take ten normal steps. Choose a spot where you're unlikely to be interrupted, like a trail farther back from the parking lot.

Find ten stones or other kind of marker. Pace out ten steps, and put a marker at each step. Stand at the first mark so you're facing the others in a straight line in front of you.

If you feel comfortable doing it, take off your shoes and socks. As we talked about in the Touch chapter, barefoot walking will deepen your sensory perceptions. That connection will in turn further chase away anxious thoughts.

Next, use progressive muscle relaxation to release as much tension as you can. Do your best to calm your body.

Lower your eyes so you only see the first few stones in front of you. You need to see the stones so you know where to walk, but you want to minimize visual distraction.

Take a few deep, calming breaths. Then take your first step.

As you walk from stone to stone, do your best not to think. Let those everyday thoughts flow out of your mind.

When I meditate, I've come to view my thoughts as ocean waves. I form a mental picture of the ocean, then visualize smoothing it until it's as calm and flat as glass.

If that image helps you, use it. If not, another focusing technique is to repeat a sentence with each step. Something simple like, "Now I let go of all my worries" works well, but it can be any positive statement.

With each step, your mind will wander. You'll find yourself thinking something like, "This is stupid. What am I doing? Did I leave the oven on? The garage door open? Will I finish that spreadsheet on time?"

Push those thoughts away. Replace them with the immediate sensations around you, like the temperature of the ground against your feet.

When you reach the end of your line of stones, pause. Take a few deep breaths. Reflect. Then turn around and start back to the beginning. Keep repeating your statement with each step.

If you can, do this meditation for ten minutes. When you're ready, take a few final deep breaths, put your shoes back on, and head back rejuvenated into the world.

A walking meditation can work anywhere, but my favorite place to do this practice is at the beach. The tactile sensations of bare feet on sand alongside the white noise of waves are particularly good at pushing away anxiety-induced ruminations. Photo: Zack Minor on Unsplash

Chapter 13

GIVING BACK

I want to realize brotherhood or identity not merely with the beings called human, but I want to realize identity with all life, even with such beings as crawl on earth.
– Mahatma Gandhi

When you engage in Deep Nature Observation, you cannot help but fall in love with the places and life you observe. The details you notice, the insights you gain, and the unexpected finds you discover all forge an emotional bond between you and the natural world.

With this bond can come profound sadness, an overwhelming feeling of loss. Throughout this book I've emphasized the joy and vibrancy of nature, and to be sure, much of that beauty remains. But for the deep nature observer, that beauty also reminds us how much we've lost in the pursuit of so-called "progress."

Human are impossible to miss when engaging in Deep Nature Observation. Invasive plants like multiflora rose choke out undergrowth. Non-native insects like emerald ash borer decimate species. Even ticks have increased their range beyond natural levels thanks to climate change.

You'll also feel humanity's impacts in what you don't observe. American chestnuts once dominated eastern North American forests. Now I count myself lucky if I see a tiny sapling, struggling in vain against the imported chestnut blight.

Our fields and woods have become quieter. Rachel Carson's horrific prediction of a silent spring may yet come to pass. A 2019 study in the journal *Science* found that since 1970, the songbird population in the United States and Canada has dropped by 2.9 billion—nearly a 30 percent loss.[1] Grassland birds alone have lost more than half their population in just 50 years.

I have seen people who care deeply about the natural world fall into despair at these losses. Sometimes it seems the only thing we can do to nature is harm it.

While I understand why people feel that way, I don't agree with it. I went to college to become a forester. In forestry, we learn that yes, we humans have the capacity to harm nature. But we also have the ability to reverse that damage.

I've seen these improvements first-hand. When I left school and began working with woodland owners, I met people committed to making their properties better for the plants and animals that lived there. Their work inspired me to write two books about land stewardship in the hope that other landowners would take up the challenge.

This chapter is my similar challenge to you. Maybe you have a backyard. Maybe you live in an apartment building and don't own any land at all. That's all right. Just like you don't need to own land to observe nature, you don't need to own land to improve your local landscape.

This chapter isn't some squishy reminder to "take care of the planet." In keeping with the rest of the book, I've focused this chapter on local, on-the-ground actions you can take to benefit nature.

PLANT A TREE

Perhaps it's cliché to talk about planting a tree in a chapter on giving back to nature, but it's worth the discussion. Planting a tree is one of the simplest yet most powerful ways you can benefit nature in your community.

Adding a tree to your yard helps green your neighborhood. And when lots of people plant trees, it can change the character of a city.

While bird populations have dropped across habitats, grassland birds like this eastern meadowlark have seen especially steep drops due to loss of habitat. Photo: Jake Bonello, U.S. Fish and Wildlife Service

In areas with a lot of deer, you may need to protect newly planted trees with fencing or tree tubes. Tree tubes, like those pictured here, keep animals from munching a tree and can speed up its early growth. If you plant with a community group, the group may provide tree tubes and installation instructions. Author photo

Cities and neighborhoods with more trees tend to have lower crime and higher incomes. Trees also filter the air and reduce incidents of asthma. They reduce urban heat and make cities more comfortable to live in.

If you don't have space in your backyard to plant a tree, connect with your local parks department or the owners of whatever place you like to explore outdoors. They can often use help from volunteers to plant trees in their parks, forests, and natural areas.

Whether planting a tree in your yard or in a park, you'll likely plant "container stock" trees—a fancy way of saying the tree will come in a pot. Container trees come in many ages and sizes, but the planting method is similar for all of them.

First, dig a hole as deep as the pot the tree came in and two to three times as wide. Next, remove the tree from the container by grasping near the trunk's base and pulling. If the tree doesn't come out easily, use a utility knife to cut the pot on two sides and peel it away.

The tree's roots will often become tightly bound inside the pot. Resist the temptation to cut them. Doing that will injure the tree. Instead, break up the soil using your hands. This gives the roots space to grow without damaging them.

Don't toss that potting soil either. Use it in the hole you dug. It will give the tree extra nutrients and make planting easier.

Put your tree in the hole. The top of the root ball should be about an inch above the ground.

A small section of the pine forest my father helped plant back in his youth. One of the most satisfying aspects of working in nature and of planting trees is seeing how that work makes a difference even decades later. Author photo

Make sure the trunk stands up straight. Before filling in the hole with soil, adjust the tree as needed to remove any lean.

When you fill in the hole, use your foot to tamp down the soil. This will push out air pockets and promote root-to-soil contact.

Water your tree right after planting. A good, soaking rain within 24 hours of planting also works. You want the soil moist, not soggy.

Skip fertilizer. Trees do just fine with the native soil.

If you want to mulch, leave a gap between the mulch and the tree. Mulching right up to the trunk can cause the tree to rot.

Planting a tree like this doesn't just benefit nature. It benefits you.

Growing up, I remember walking with my father through a pine forest in central Pennsylvania. My father led me through this forest for quite a ways before he looked at me with a smile and said, "Did you know I planted these trees?"

I was astonished. The trees were so tall. It looked like a forest that had been there forever, but it hadn't.

When my father was a kid, the area had been a field. He and a group of other kids had helped the property owner plant thousands of trees. Forty years later, the tiny seedlings they'd planted had grown into a vibrant forest that supported a rich diversity of plants and wildlife.

I know my father felt a surge of pride seeing those trees and the way his work had literally grown with time. You'll feel that same pride when you visit your tree and see how much it's grown. The bigger your tree gets, the more satisfaction you'll feel knowing that tree is there thanks to your action. It's an amazing legacy to hand down to future generations.

JOIN A LOCAL FRIENDS GROUP OR LAND TRUST

In many ways, Deep Nature Observation is an escape. It's a way we can take a break and reset our minds, bodies, senses, and spirits.

But as I hope you've learned over the course of this book, Deep Nature Observation is also about connection. It brings us closer to the natural world. And in caring for that world, it can draw you closer to other people as well.

I've had the good fortune to experience this firsthand. In more than fifteen years working in various outdoor jobs, I've had the pleasure of getting to know hundreds of staff at local park departments, state and federal government agencies, and non-profit land trusts. They're the hardest-working, most dedicated professionals I've ever met.

Odds are, some of these same passionate people live and work near you. Thousands of small, local, outdoor-focused groups exist throughout the world. Many work in one state, region, city, or even park.

Many larger parks, like state and national parks, have their own dedicated non-profit organizations that help with maintenance. These are usually known as "Friends" groups since they often have names

Parks and nature preserves are beautiful places, but they take a lot of hard work to stay that way. Supporting a local Friends group or land trust can help nature in your community. Photo: Ries Bosch on Unsplash

like "Friends of Memorial Park." Your local parks may have a similar organization.

Finding these groups can be a challenge. Most have few staff. Many are completely volunteer-run. Advertising budgets usually hover around zero.

So how do you locate these groups? One place to start is an Internet search for the name of your local park or nature preserve. Often you'll find the organization or government agency who manages it. Their website may have contact information and may even point you toward a partnering non-profit that helps with maintenance.

Local chapters of larger organizations like the Nature Conservancy and the Audubon Society are also good places to begin. You can find chapter information on both groups' websites. Even if you don't want to join a bigger group, the staff at these organizations will often be aware of and involved with other local organizations.

Another method to find local groups is the Land Trust Alliance's "Find a Land Trust" tool (www. findalandtrust.org). It can connect you with more than a thousand non-profit land protection organizations.

Land trusts are good groups to connect with for three reasons. First, they exist to conserve land. They often own nature preserves that allow public access, so they can help you discover new places to explore. Second, these groups frequently host educational events like workshops and guided hikes. Third, these groups routinely need volunteers to help them care for the properties they own. You may

The staff and volunteers that support public lands are dedicated, phenomenal people. Get to know the groups in your area that care for your favorite outdoor spaces. Photo: National Park Service

Culverts like this one need periodic maintenance to function. Left alone, culverts can get plugged with debris after storms. If a culvert isn't maintained, water will back up and eventually blow out the trail. Author photo

be able to find opportunities to help with the stewardship projects I describe next.

HELP MAINTAIN YOUR LOCAL PARK

Once you've found these groups, how can you help them? While financial donations are of course always useful, what many groups need most are volunteers.

As dedicated as park and recreation professionals are, they still struggle to care for parks, forests, and nature preserves under their care. It isn't because they're lazy. It's simply a monumental task.

The COVID-19 pandemic drove home that reality. Outdoor recreation boomed during the pandemic as other recreation options closed.

Public lands saw a surge in visitors. That was amazing, but it also led to a lot of maintenance. Trail erosion, overflowing trash cans, invasive plants…the list goes on.

Many parks departments and non-profit organizations work on small budgets. In the case of local parks, they frequently rely on public works staff for maintenance. Those staff often have responsibilities well beyond just the parks.

All this to say: public lands need volunteers. Professional staff can guide volunteer work, but they need support to keep public lands in good shape for visitors.

That's where you come in. The best way to give back to the places where you engage in Deep Nature Observation is to volunteer with the organization that owns or maintains that place.

For whatever reason, mice and squirrels like to gnaw on plastic trail markers. You can see rodent damage on this blue trail marker. If the marker isn't replaced, the damage can worsen to the point where the marker will fall off. Author photo

What kind of work will you do as a volunteer? The needs are as endless as the parks and nature preserves out there. Tree planting is a big one, which we already talked about. Standard maintenance help like picking up trash or cleaning facilities is another.

Trail upkeep is a third common need. Trails see heavy use from visitors, and all that traffic compresses the surface. When it rains, water rushes along this compacted ground. Over time, that fast-moving water washes away the trail.

A common way parks and forests protect their trails from this damage is by installing water control devices in the trail itself. These devices come in several designs based on the amount and type of traffic a trail receives. Professionals usually install these devices since they frequently need equipment like bulldozers. But as a volunteer, you might help remove the debris that builds up in them, like leaves and sticks that can clog culverts.

Another common trail maintenance activity is keeping trail markers in good shape. Whatever markers your local park uses, they will need replacement at some point. Painted blazes fade. Rodents chew on plastic markers. Stone piles fall down.

Losing one or two trail markers may not seem like a big deal. But on backwoods trails, hikers could get lost.

When you're out on a trail, note any missing, damaged, or faded markers. Connect with the park's staff, Friends group, or land trust to get those markers repaired during an upcoming cleanup day.

PULL INVASIVE PLANTS

Another common volunteer task is removing invasive plants. These non-native plants can take over a park or nature preserve.

The trouble with invasive plants is that if you don't know what you're looking at, your local park can seem healthy when it really isn't. Beautiful green shrubs fill the open space below the trees. Thousands of fragrant flowers and juicy berries dot those shrubs, giving the park a burst of color.

But those same shrubs can devastate your local preserve. They choke off the native wildflowers, shrubs, and young trees that should be growing. In turn, there's less food for wildlife to eat, because many wildlife can only eat native plants.

Invasive plants are especially challenging for park managers to deal with because they spread so rapidly. You control invasives in one area, and they pop up somewhere else. Worse, even if you do pull them, they often regrow, creating an ongoing maintenance need.

The best way I've found to deal with invasive plants in a local park is to assemble a group of volunteers. You then work as a team to remove as many of the plants as possible in a single effort.

The tools and techniques you'll use to deal with invasive plants will vary depending on what plants you're dealing with. Suffice to say here, the best option is to talk to your Friends group and join a volunteer cleanup day. The group or the parks department will typically supply you with gear and instructions. They'll also be able to help with plant identification so you don't accidentally yank a rare orchid while you're ripping out invasives.

EXPLORE AN OUTDOOR CAREER

If you find you enjoy volunteering in the outdoors, it's possible to go further. You can pursue a career in nature as well.

I can say, without question, that working in the outdoor field has been the most rewarding experience of my life. Planting a tree makes a difference for decades to come. Doing that work every day, you literally see the difference you make. Forests that are healthier because of better management. Lands that

These woods in my local park in central Pennsylvania may seem lush, but they're a wildlife wasteland thanks to heavy infestations of invasive plants like oriental bittersweet and bush honeysuckle. Author photo

are forever protected because of a conservation easement. Well-maintained trails, ballfields, and playgrounds that will inspire future outdoor lovers.

When many people walk in their parks, they don't realize the hard work it takes to keep so-called "open space" in good shape. In turn, they don't realize the many career options in the great outdoors. Park managers, foresters, planners, land protection specialists, groundskeepers…I could keep this list going and going.

Some of these careers require college degrees. If you're thinking about college and college majors, consider programs like natural resource management, forestry, or recreation and tourism.

If college isn't your thing, that's ok too. Parks and forests can always use those with technical skills like equipment operators and mechanics.

What if you've already finished school, and you don't want to go back? Consider positions that may not have you outdoors directly, but that support those working in parks and forests.

Many land trusts and park agencies need employees in IT, communications, HR, accounting, and legal. These support positions often go unfilled because people in those fields don't realize these opportunities exist.

To be fair, looking for outdoor jobs can be a challenge. Since many parks and land trusts have small teams, it's hard to find jobs with them through big employment sites.

Several professional associations provide starting points. They have

When people think of outdoor careers, often they think the only option is a park ranger. Rangers are amazing! But there are lots of other career options in the outdoors that you can explore as well. Photo: National Park Service

job boards, and they also have resources about career options, suggested degree programs, and continuing education courses.

Check out these groups if you want to learn more about careers in nature:

- **National Recreation and Parks Association**
  www.nrpa.org
- **North American Association for Environmental Education**
  www.naaee.org
- **Society of American Foresters**
  www.eforester.org
- **The Wildlife Society**
  www.wildlife.org

As amazing as these groups are, the best way I've found to get involved professionally in the outdoors has been the old-school way: networking. As you volunteer and get to know your local organizations and park agencies, you'll start to hear about positions that open up.

You'll also get clued into local job boards for conservation organizations. Many states have their own land trust advocacy groups. Many have similar organizations for parks and recreation. These organizations will frequently have job boards that local groups post to.

Above all, if you're interested in an outdoor career, talk to someone who already works in that field. As I've said, these folks are passionate about their jobs. Many could have gotten higher paying work in other industries. They chose this path because it matters deeply, often

Public land agencies receive minuscule fractions of government spending, yet they safeguard many of our most important natural, historic, and cultural sites. The Flight 93 Memorial, managed by the National Park Service, is just one example. Photo: C. Claycomb, National Park Service

personally, to them. Most will be beyond thrilled to talk with you about their professional journeys and offer advice on how you can follow your dream to an outdoor career.

ADVOCATE FOR PUBLIC LANDS

To be honest, I can't believe I need to include this section. For me, the benefits of parks, forests, trails, nature preserves, and other public lands are blatantly obvious. And their cost? Pennies compared with what else governments spend tax dollars on.

I'm speaking literally with that last sentence. Consider the National Park Service. They oversee

Public lands belong to all of us, and they include more than national parks. Many of the public lands targeted for sale in the Big Beautiful Bill draft were managed by lesser known agencies like the U.S. Bureau of Land Management, which oversees this site, Red Cliffs National Conservation Area. Photo: Bob Wick, Bureau of Land Management

Yellowstone, the Grand Canyon, and more than 400 other sites across the U.S. Some of them are among the country's most hallowed places, like the USS Arizona in Hawaii and the Flight 93 Memorial in my home state of Pennsylvania.

These sites are incredibly popular. More than 331 million people visited national park units in 2024 alone.[2] That's not only a record, it's nearly equal to the entire U.S. population.

Despite that, the National Park Service budget is less than 0.1 percent of the federal budget.

Think about that. For every federal tax dollar spent, less than a tenth of a penny goes to support these incredible spaces.

It's the same in countless states and cities across the U.S. And while I can't speak for other countries, I would guess it's the same elsewhere. It's a shame, because as we've seen, nature is an ally in our fight against many societal challenges, from obesity to mental health.

And yet, there remain those who say we spend too much on public land. Worse, there are those who question whether we should have public land at all.

In past years, big stories have hit the U.S. news about oil drilling in the Arctic National Wildlife Refuge, or ANWR. Admittedly, those stories are easy to tune out. ANWR is in remote Alaska. Nearly all Americans will never visit it. Even a nature lover like me will probably never go there.

But this threat to public land isn't limited to far-off wildernesses. Some politicians from local to state to federal are openly hostile to the idea of public land. They'd rather sell it off for a quick buck.

Think that would never happen? In the U.S., it nearly just did.

In 2025, the U.S. Congress passed what was popularly called the "One Big Beautiful Bill Act." A draft of that bill would have allowed the U.S. government to sell millions of acres of public land and put it into private hands for development.[3]

Thanks to intense, bipartisan pressure, that provision got cut from the final bill.

But if you think that's the end of it, think again. Those who would take away our public lands and sell them off are still around. They won't give up. Silence guarantees their victory.

This isn't a partisan cause. Public lands aren't a Democrat issue or a Republican issue. Our public parks, forests, and trails belong to all of us. They're economic drivers for rural communities. They're health and wellness powerhouses. They filter our air and clean our water. And at a time of intense political polarization, they're a shared part of our identity and heritage no matter where we come from or who we vote for.

So at whatever level you feel comfortable, I hope you become a champion for public lands. For

It isn't just federal land that needs support. State and local parks are often targets for politicians looking to cut expenses. They call them luxuries. But something the COVID pandemic made abundantly clear: parks and public lands are every bit the essential infrastructure that highways and bridges are. They're crucial to our physical and mental well-being and to the healthy development of our children. Photo: Oakville Dude on Unsplash

providing enough funding to maintain them. For keeping public lands in public hands. And for seeking opportunities to create new parks and nature preserves.

That last one is critical. Many people still lack close-to-home outdoor recreation opportunities. Not everyone can afford to fly or drive to a national park. Local and state parks are just as crucial to make sure everyone can experience the joy and wonder of the outdoors.

Maybe it's a call or letter to your elected officials. Maybe it's who you vote for in elections. Maybe it's an editorial in the local news or a post on social media. Parks can't speak for themselves. Speak on their behalf.

With screens everywhere, it's never been harder to get kids outside. But we need to do it if we want them to care for nature and public land after we're gone. Photo: Hessam Nabavi on Unsplash

INSPIRE THE NEXT GENERATION OF OUTDOOR STEWARDS

You've likely heard former U.S. President Ronald Reagan's line, "Freedom is never more than one generation away from extinction." It comes from his 1967 inaugural address when he became governor of California.

The quote continues, "It is not ours by way of inheritance; it must be fought for and defended constantly by each generation, for it comes only once to a people. And those in world history who have known freedom and then lost it have never known it again."

More and more, I feel like you could substitute the words "public land" or "nature" in that statement.

As another famous saying goes, they aren't making more land. Once it's gone, once it's sold, once it's developed, that's it. Returning that land to any kind of natural state becomes extremely hard.

And as we just saw, the fact that a piece of land is designated a national forest, or wildlife refuge, or whatever else, doesn't guarantee its protection. That protection comes from laws. Other laws can take it away.

As important as it is for us to defend public land now, that's only the short-term debate. To protect these places for the future, we need to think beyond our own generation. We need to think about

Something else revealing about that study of kids in nature? Age-related declines in time outside start earlier in girls than in boys. And for both boys and girls, increases happened only when kids started engaging in nature before age five. The earlier you can start exposing the kids in your life to nature, especially girls, the more likely they are to continue enjoying the outdoors later in life. Photo: Gabby Orcutt on Unsplash

how we connect young people with nature and inspire them to care for it when we no longer can.

I'm afraid the statistics on that aren't great. With screentime more compelling than ever, it's never been harder to get kids outside.

The good news, though, is that we have the power to change that.

In 2023, an analysis of 55 studies examined the factors that led kids to spend more time outdoors. The combined studies looked at 119 possible factors.

Among the factors that led to more time outside? Parental involvement. Parents who made a habit of getting outside with their kids had kids who went on to spend more time outside

as they got older.[4]

It didn't matter the parents' background. Education, income, occupation, ethnicity…none of them made a difference.

Even if you don't think of yourself as "outdoorsy," you can still inspire the kids in your life to spend more time outside. All you have to do is take them.

I hope this book helps you with that. I designed most of the skills and Try This exercises as solo activities. But they don't have to be. Nearly all of them can happen with a family member or a group, and most are kid-friendly.

Will doing a few outdoor activities with kids really make a difference?

For our last Try This, here's one that works perfectly on a family trip.

To do it, I need to take you back to ye olden times and the days of *(gasp!)* actual film in cameras.

Imagine you're in a park or nature preserve. You're far from your car when you look down at your camera and realize, to your horror, that you have only one picture left.

If you can't remember the days of actual film, imagine instead that your camera or phone is down to one percent battery. One more picture is all it will take for it to turn off.

A Last Picture doesn't have to be a grand landscape. It can be something small, like this waterfall in a stream. Whatever is meaningful to you in your memory of that place. Author photo

What one picture would you take of that place, if you could only take one?

Would you choose some iconic landscape, like an overlook or waterfall? Maybe you would pick something intimate, like a flower that caught your eye. Maybe you'd do a group shot with your family.

There's no right or wrong answer. The point is that whatever you choose for your Last Picture, it says a lot about you, the place, and the connection between you.

A Last Picture is a great activity when visiting an outdoor place with a group. As you walk, when you choose your Last Picture, hold out your hands so they form a rectangle. That rectangle is the "frame" for your picture. If you want, you can actually take the shot with your camera.

Afterward, talk with the group about why you chose that scene. When they've taken their Last Pictures, listen to why they picked what they did.

I'm sure each of you will pick something at least a little different. What will your choices reveal about you and the people you're with?

Here's what I hope they reveal. I hope they reveal that you've come to appreciate the outdoor spaces around you. I hope they reveal that you've learned to see beyond the obvious in nature and look deeply at the world.

Most importantly, I hope they reveal that your time outside has brought you closer to nature and the people you care about. That was the whole point of this book. If even one activity in here has helped you make those connections, then I consider all the work I put into writing these words worth it.

I can say with certainty that it can. Talk to almost anyone who works in an outdoor career today. Ask them why they decided to pursue that career. Nearly every one of them will tell you about a parent, relative, teacher, or other adult in their life got them outside.

For me, it was my dad. He took me camping when I was a kid. From the moment I first saw the stars—really saw them on a dark night—I was hooked.

Sometimes that's all it takes. Even a single interaction can inspire a kid to learn more about nature and want to protect it.

That's it. I have nothing else to say. Why are you still indoors? Stop reading. Get outside!

After graduating college, I moved to the Catskill Mountains of upstate New York. I lived there for eight years before returning to my roots in Pennsylvania. Below is the last photo I took before I moved. It's the office of the land trust where I worked as a forester and environmental educator. The fields, forests, and mountains of the Catskills will always be part of me, and the people I worked with will be even more so. That's why I chose this shot as my Last Picture. Author photo

ENDNOTES

CHAPTER 1 - SENSORY NUMBNESS

1. See, for instance, C.M. Gigliotti and others, "Harvesting Health: Effects of Three Types of Horticultural Therapy Activities for Persons with Dementia," *Dementia: The International Journal of Social Research and Practice* 3, no. 2 (2004): 161-180. Also see Marc Berman and others, "The Cognitive Benefits of Interacting with Nature," *Psychological Science* 19, no. 12 (2008): 1207-1212.

CHAPTER 2 - WHAT IS DEEP NATURE OBSERVATION?

1. Bum Jin Park and others, "The Physiological Effects of Shinrin-yoku (Taking in the Forest Atmosphere or Forest Bathing): Evidence from Field Experiments in 24 Forests across Japan," *Environmental Health and Preventive Medicine* 15 (2010), 18-26.

2. Yoshifumi Miyazaki and others, "Forest Medicine Research in Japan," *Japanese Journal of Hygiene* 69 (2014), 122-135. See also Q. Li and others, "A Forest Bathing Trip Increases Human Natural Killer Activity and Expression of Anti-cancer Proteins in Female Subjects," *Journal of Biological Regulators and Homeostatic Agents* 22, no. 1 (2008), 45-55.

CHAPTER 3 - PREPARING TO OBSERVE

1. Jo Barton and Jules Pretty, "What Is the Best Dose of Nature and Green Exercise for Improving Mental Health? A Multi-Study Analysis," *Environmental Science and Technology* 44, no 10 (2010): 3947-3955.

CHAPTER 5 - HEARING

1. Cassandra D. Gould van Praag and others, "Mind-Wandering and Alterations to Default Mode Network Connectivity When Listening to Naturalistic Versus Artificial Sounds," *Scientific Reports*: 7, 45273 (2017).

CHAPTER 6 - SMELL

1. Jessica Morrison, "Human Nose Can Detect 1 Trillion Odors," *Nature* (2014).

2. David Nowak and others, "Tree and Forest Effects on Air Quality and Human Health in the United States," *Environmental Pollution* 193 (2014): 119-129.

3. Geoffrey Donovan and others, "The Relationship between Trees and Human Health: Evidence from the Spread of the Emerald Ash Borer," *American Journal of Preventive Medicine* 44, no. 2 (2013): 139-145.

4. B.C. Wolverton, Anne Johnson, and Keith Bounds. *Interior Landscape Plants for Indoor Air Pollution Abatement*, National Aeronautics and Space Administration, Stennis Space Center, MS, 1989. 30 p.

5. Min-sun Lee and others, "Interaction with indoor plants may reduce psychological and physiological stress by suppressing autonomic nervous system activity in young adults: a randomized crossover study," *Journal of Physiological Anthropology* 34, no. 1 (2015): 21-26.

6. Markham Heid, "You Asked: Can Indoor Plants Really Purify the Air?" *Time*, January 17, 2018, available online at http://time.com/5105027/indoor-plants-air-quality/.

7. Vanessa Perez, Dominik Alexander, and William Bailey, "Air Ions and Mood Outcomes: A Review and Meta-Analysis," *BioMed Central Psychiatry* 13 (2013): 29-48.

CHAPTER 7 - TOUCH

1. G. Chevalier and others, "Earthing: Health Implications of Reconnecting the Human Body to the Earth's Surface Electrons," 2012, *Journal of Environmental and Public Health*, available online at https://www.ncbi.nlm.nih.gov/pmc/articles/PMC3265077/pdf/JEPH2012-291541.pdf.

2. Chris Lowry and others, "Identification of an Immune-Responsive Mesolimbocortical Serotonergic System: Potential Role in Regulation of Emotional Behavior," *Neuroscience* 146 (2007): 756-772.

CHAPTER 9 - BEYOND THE FIVE

1. P.K. Piff and others, "Awe, the Small Self, and Prosocial Behavior," *Journal of Personality and Social Psychology* Vol. 108, no. 6 (2015):883-899.

CHAPTER 13 - GIVING BACK

1. K.V. Rosenburg and others, "Decline of the North American Avifauna," *Science* 366, no. 6461 (2019): 120-124.

2. National Park Service, March 5, 2025, "Visitation Numbers," www.nps.gov/aboutus/visitation-numbers.htm, accessed July 23, 2025.

3. Nik Kohomban, June 16, 2025, "Congress Is Making More Than 250 Million Acres of Public Lands Available for Sale." The Wilderness Society.

https://www.wilderness.org/articles/blog/congress-making-more-250-million-acres-public-lands-available-sale. Accessed July 5, 2025.

4. Richard Larouche and others, "Determinants of Outdoor Time in Children and Youth: A Systemic Review of Longitudinal and Intervention Studies," *International Journal of Environmental Research and Public Health* 20, no. 2 (2023): 1328, 33p.

CHAPTER START AND END PHOTO CREDITS

Chapter 1:
- Gorilla – Joshua Cotten on Unsplash

Chapter 2:
- American toad – author photo

Chapter 3:
- Owl – Geoffrey Moore on Unsplash

Chapter 4:
- Hand lens – Vasilina Sirotina on Unsplash

Chapter 5:
- Eastern towhee – author photo
- Wild turkey – Courtney Celley, U.S. Fish and Wildlife Service

Chapter 6:
- Woman meditating – Pixabay

Chapter 7:
- Touching a plant – Serjan Midili on Unsplash

Chapter 8:
- Blueberries – Juliana Marx on Unsplash

Chapter 9:
- Night sky over water – Thomas Ciszewski on Unsplash
- Person looking up at night sky – Klemen Vrankar on Unsplash

Chapter 10:
- Woman using a camera – William Warby on Unsplash

Chapter 11:
- Outdoor art – Margarita Shtyfura on Unsplash

Chapter 12:
- Woman sitting in a field – Inspa Makers on Unsplash

Chapter 13:
- Planting a seed – Vitor Monthay on Unsplash